BLOCK CHAIN INVESTING

2022

BY NFT TRENDING CRYPTO ART

"An investment in knowledge pays the best interest"

- Benjamin Franklin.

GET A FREE AUDIOBOOK

EMAIL SUBJECT LINE:

"BLOCKCHAIN"

TO

MINDSETMASTERSHIP@GMAIL.COM

JOIN OUR

NFT, CRYPTO ART,

METAVERSE & DEFI

Entrepreneur Power Group

To help reinforce the learning's from our books, I strongly suggest you join our well-informed powerhouse community on Facebook.

Here, you will connect and share with other like-minded people to support your journey and help you grow.

>>>CLICK BELOW to join Our NFT Group <<<

News Site & Community Group:

https://www.facebook.com/groups/nfttrending/

Want Future Book Releases?

Email us at:

mindsetmastership@gmail.com

Find us on Instagram!

@MindsetMastership

MASTERSHIP BOOKS

UK | USA | Canada | Ireland | Australia

India | New Zealand | South Africa | China

Mastership Books is part of the United Arts Publishing House group of companies based in London, England, UK.

First published by Mastership Books (London, UK), 2022

I S B N: 978-1-915002-28-0

Text Copyright © United Arts Publishing

Cover design by Rich © United Arts Publishing (UK)
Text and internal design by Rich © United Arts Publishing (UK)
Image credits reserved.
Colour separation by Spitting Image Design Studio
Printed and bound in Great Britain
National Publications Association of Britain
London, England, United Kingdom.
Paper design UAP
ISBN: 978-1-915002-28-0

(paperback)

A723.5

Title: **Blockchain Investing**

Design, Bound & Printed:

London, England,

Great Britain.

"If you really want to invest in something today, start investing your knowledge in **NFTs**, **Metaverse** and **DeFi**, these hidden treasure are going mainstream"

Contents

INTRODUCTION

Basics of Blockchain Technology
Meaning of Blockchain

Blockchain technology is a network of P2P nodes, also known as blocks, that keeps transactional records of the public in different databases, known as the chain. This type of storage is sometimes referred to as a digital ledger. Each transaction in this ledger is signed with the owner's digital signature, verifying the transaction and protecting it from manipulation. Consequently, the data in the digital ledger is highly secured.

Evolution of Blockchain Technology

Although Blockchain is a relatively young technology, it has a long and fascinating history. The following is a chronology of some of the most significant and well-known events in the history of Blockchain technology.

2008

Bitcoin, a P2P electronic cash system, was released in 2008 by Satoshi Nakamoto, a pseudonym for a person or group.

2009

The first successful Bitcoin (BTC) transaction was made in 2009 by computer scientist Hal Finney and the creative developer Satoshi Nakamoto.

2010

In 2010, Laszlo Hanycez, a Florida programmer, made the first Bitcoin purchase – two Papa John's pizzas. Hanycez sent 10,000 BTC, worth about $60 at the time. At the time, the value of a transaction was usually negotiated on the Bitcoin forum, a discussion a chat platform.

2011

The cryptocurrency was tied to the US dollar in 2011, with 1 BTC equaling $1. During this period, the Electronic Frontier Foundation (an NGO dedicated to preserving civil liberties in the digital space), Wikileaks, and other organizations started to accept Bitcoin as payment.

2012

During this epoch of Blockchain development, the Good Wife (a TV series) covered Blockchain and cryptocurrencies, incorporating Blockchain into mainstream culture. Bitcoin Magazine was founded by Vitalik Buterin, an early Bitcoin developer.

2013

In 2013, the market capitalization of BTC surpassed $1 billion. Bitcoin reached a price of $100 per BTC for the first time. Vitalik Buterin also launched the Ethereum Project during this period. Experts suggest that, aside from Bitcoin, Blockchain may have other applications (e.g., smart contracts, which have become a crucial component of decentralization).

2014

In 2014, Zynga, The D Las Vegas Hotel, and Overstock.com all began accepting Bitcoin as payment. Similarly, Buterin crowdfunded his Ethereum project via an Initial Coin Offering (ICO), which raised more than $18 million in Bitcoin and opened up new Blockchain opportunities. R3, a collaboration of over 200 Blockchain companies, was formed to identify novel ways to deploy Blockchain technology. PayPal also announced the addition of Bitcoin to its platform.

2015

In 2015, the number of retailers accepting Bitcoin hit 100,000. The NASDAQ and Chain, a San Francisco-based Blockchain startup, collaborated to investigate the technology for trading shares in private companies.

2016

IBM launched a Blockchain strategy for corporate cloud applications. Also, the Japanese government recognizes Blockchain and cryptocurrency as legitimate at the time. On February 23, the Financial Services Agency of Japan presented legal revisions to recognize Bitcoin and other cryptocurrencies as fiat money.

2017

In 2017, Bitcoin surpassed $1,000/BTC for the first time. Cryptocurrency market capitalization topped $150 billion. JP Morgan CEO Jamie Dimon claimed that Blockchain is a future technology, signaling that Wall Street believes in the ledger system. Bitcoin reaches an all-time high of $19,783.21/BTC. Also, Dubai stated that its administration will be Blockchain-based by 2020.

2018

Facebook announced the formation of a Blockchain group and hinted at the possibility of establishing its token. Also, Citi and Barclays, amongst other large banks, signed on to IBM's Blockchain-based financial infrastructure.

2019

China's President Ji Xinping openly backed Blockchain, and the country's central bank announced its intention to build its cryptocurrency. According to Twitter and Square CEO Jack Dorsey, Square stated its plan to hire Blockchain experts to work on its future crypto goals. The New York Stock Exchange (NYSE) also announced the introduction of Bakkt, a cryptocurrency trading platform and digital wallet.

2020

PayPal announced that its users could buy, sell, and store Bitcoins on its platform. The Bahamas stated its plan to issue digital money known as the Sand Dollar. In the fight against COVID-19, Blockchain played a significant role, primarily in storing medical research data and patient information.

Blockchain Transaction Process

A crucial aspect of Blockchain technology is how it confirms and authorizes transactions. If two people want to carry out a transaction with their private and public keys, the first person will attach the transaction information to the public key of the second person. This complete collection of information has been gathered into a single block. The block contains a digital signature, a timestamp, and other critical, essential information. It's worth mentioning that the block doesn't include the person's identity in the transaction. The system forwards this block via all of the network's nodes, and the transaction is complete when the correct user matches his private key to the block. In addition to cash transactions, the Blockchain might hold transactional data for houses, automobiles, and other things.

Hash Encryptions

Hashing and encryption safeguard data in Blockchain technology, with the SHA256 method being the most used. The SHA256 algorithm delivers the sender's address (public key), the receiver's address, the transaction, and personal data. The encrypted data, known as hash encryption, is sent worldwide and verified before being added to the Blockchain. The SHA256 technique makes hash encryption almost hard to crack, making sender and recipient authentication much more accessible.

Proof of Work

Each block in a Blockchain has significant headers.

- Previous Hash: This hash address refers to the block before it.

- Transaction Data: This carries the information on all transactions that must occur.

- Nonce: Nonce is an arbitrary number used in cryptography to distinguish the hash address of a block.

The system sends all of the above (i.e., the previous hash, transaction data, and nonce) using a hashing method, producing an output with a 256-bit, a 64-character-long value known as the unique 'hash address.' As a result, it's referred to as the block's hash. Many individuals use computer procedures to find the appropriate hash value to fulfill a pre-determined criterion. When the predefined condition is satisfied, the transaction is complete. Put another way, Blockchain miners are attempting to solve a mathematical riddle known as a proof of work problem, and the first person to solve it receives a prize.

Mining

Mining is the process of adding transactional information to the current digital/public ledger in Blockchain technology. Though it is most often connected with Bitcoin, other Blockchain transactions use the phrase. Mining entails creating a difficult-to-forge hash of a block transaction, maintaining the security of the whole Blockchain without the need for a governance system.

Elements of the Blockchain
Immutable record

No one can alter or tamper with a transaction after entering it into the shared ledger. If there is an error in a transaction record, a new transaction is created to remove the error, and both transactions must be available.

Distributed ledgers technology

All network users can access the distributed ledger and its immutable record of transactions. Using this shared ledger, transactions are only recorded once, minimizing the frequent duplication of transactions in traditional corporate networks.

Smart contracts

Smart contracts are a collection of rules stored on the Blockchain and executed automatically to speed up transactions. A smart contract can establish corporate bond transfer conditions and travel insurance payment terms.

Mechanism of the Blockchain Technology

Each transaction is logged as a block of data as each transaction occurs. The movement of a physical (a product) or intangible (intellectual) asset is shown in these transactions. You may record whatever data you want in the data block. This may include who, what, when, where, how much, and even the cargo status, such as temperature.

Each block is linked to the ones before it and those after it. These blocks form a data chain as assets move from one location to another or ownership changes. The blocks are securely linked together to prevent any block from being modified or added between two other blocks, and they authenticate the precise time and sequence of transactions.

Transactions are blocked together in an irreversible chain, a distributed ledger system. Each subsequent block confirms the verification of the previous block and hence the Blockchain. As a result, the Blockchain becomes tamper-evident, providing it with the critical feature of immutability. This reduces the possibility of a hostile actor manipulating your data and generating a secure transaction record for you and other network users.

Types of Blockchain Network

A Blockchain network may be built in various ways, and it can be public, private, permissioned, or developed by a group of people.

Public Blockchain Networks

A public Blockchain, such as Bitcoin, allows everyone to contribute and join. Significant computing power is required, transactions have little or no privacy and weak security. These are critical factors to consider for Blockchain application in the industry.

Private Blockchain Networks

Like a public Blockchain network, a private Blockchain network is a decentralized peer-to-peer network. However, the network is administered by a single organization that decides who is eligible to participate, conducts a consensus method, and maintains the shared ledger. This can dramatically boost participant trust and confidence, depending on the use case. You can use a private Blockchain within a company's firewall and even hosted on-premises.

Blockchain Consortiums

You can share the maintenance of a Blockchain across several organizations. A consortium Blockchain is ideal when all members must be granted authorization and share responsibilities for the Blockchain.

Permissioned Blockchain Networks

Businesses that construct a private Blockchain set up a permissioned Blockchain network. It's important to note that public Blockchain networks can be permissioned, limiting who can participate in the network and what transactions they can perform. Participants must first receive an invitation or authorization to participate.

Blockchain Versions

There are three variations of Blockchain, as shown below:

Cryptocurrency (Blockchain 1.0)

In 2005, Hall Finley released Blockchain Version 1.0, which included DLT (Distributed Ledger Technology) and the first Cryptocurrency application. It allows you to execute financial transactions using Blockchain technology or DTL and Bitcoin. This version is permissionless, which means that any participant can carry out a genuine Bitcoin transaction. The most common applications of this type are currency and payments.

Smart Contracts (Blockchain 2.0)

Smart contracts are a type of contract that can be executed on a Blockchain. The new Blockchain version was built in response to an issue in version 1.0. In version 1.0, mining Bitcoin was wasteful, and there was also a lack of network scalability and version 2.0 addressed this problem. This edition's Blockchain covers not only Cryptocurrencies but also smart contracts.

As a result, small contracts function as small computers in block chains. These small computers are free computer programs that check for requirements such as facilitation, verification, and enforcement and lower transaction costs. Ethereum has taken the position of Bitcoin in Blockchain 2.0. As a result, Blockchain 2.0 could easily manage many transactions on the public network.

DApps(Blockchain 3.0)

Following version 2.0, a new version incorporated DApps or Decentralized Applications. A DApp is similar to a standard app in that it can have any language frontend and the backend, and the backend code operates on a decentralized peer-to-peer network. It uses decentralized storage and communication technologies like Ethereum Swarm and others. Examples of decentralized applications include BitMessage, BitTorrent, Tor, Popcorn, etc.

Blockchain Architecture

A node is a person or computer that possesses a full copy of the Blockchain ledger. A block is a data structure used to store a series of transactions, and a transaction is the smallest component of a Blockchain network (records, information, etc.).

The following are the main components of the Blockchain architecture:

Node

Within the Blockchain architecture, a node is a user or a computer (each has an independent copy of the whole Blockchain ledger)

Transaction

The smallest building unit of a Blockchain system (records, information, and so on) that serves the Blockchain's purpose.

Block

A block is a data structure that stores a collection of transactions and distributes them to all nodes in a network.

Chain

A chain is a set of blocks arranged in a specified order.

Miners

Miners have dedicated nodes that execute block verification before adding anything to the Blockchain structure.

Consensus

Consensus (consensus protocol) is a collection of rules and agreements that govern how you execute Blockchain transactions.

Working Principle of Blocks

A new block is created each time a new record or transaction is added to the Blockchain. After that, each record is verified and digitally signed to confirm its authenticity. This block should be validated by most of the system's nodes before being uploaded to the network.

Let's look at what makes up a Blockchain block. Each Blockchain block is made up of the following components:

- Certain data
- The hash of the block

- The hash from the previous block

The kind of Blockchain determines the data recorded in each block. The block in the Bitcoin Blockchain structure, for example, stores information on the recipient, sender, and amount of currency.

Important Blockchain Products

There are a lot of practical applications available! If you're trying to understand the Blockchain sector, there are several places to start.

Bitcoin

Bitcoin serves as the foundation and inspiration for all Blockchain systems. Many popular platforms, like Litecoin and Dogecoin, are basic BTC derivatives.

Ethereum

The second-largest Blockchain platform is Ethereum. It's comparable to Bitcoin in some aspects, but it was envisioned as a more flexible alternative to Bitcoin, developed primarily as money. Ethereum was created to be another Internet-style network or world computer—it includes its programming language (Solidity) that allows you to write any software on the Ethereum network. Decentralized applications, or dapps, are such programs that are (theoretically) immune to central governance and monitoring.

Difference Between Bitcoin and ethereum Blockchain

Bitcoin and Ethereum are public, decentralized peer-to-peer networks with Bitcoins and Ether tokens. Both employ digital ledger technology and rely on encryption. However, their functions and capabilities are vastly different. Bitcoin is a digital currency and a decentralized payment mechanism, and its Blockchain is a database that keeps record of all Bitcoin transactions and who owns them. Ethereum is more than just a payment system; it also allows for creating smart contracts and apps, making it a more advanced Blockchain.

Stellar

Stellar was founded in 2014, two years after Bitcoin but before Ethereum. Stellar employs a more environmentally friendly synchronization method than either platform. It was built primarily for remittances and payments; thus, it has "cashlike" (i.e., extremely small) waits between transactions and is more or less free to use (transactions cost way less than a penny). Stellar, like Ethereum, lets you create additional assets (such as a digital version of a dollar or a peso) and exchange them inside the network exceptionally quickly.

Blockchain Uses Cases

Supply chain, healthcare, retail, media and advertising, financial services, insurance, travel and transportation, oil and gas, and gaming are all industries that employ Blockchain technology.

We have compiled a few potential applications below:

Cryptocurrencies

Internet money is today's 'killer app' for Blockchains. Cryptocurrencies allow you to send money across borders more quickly and cheaply than you can with a bank. Polkadot (DOT), NEO, Cardano (ADA), Tether (USDT), Binance Coin (BNB), and Litecoin are some examples of cryptocurrencies aside from traditional crypto like Bitcoin and Ethereum (LTC).

Decentralized Banking

Blockchain technology is increasingly being used in banking. Many banks, including Barclays, Canadian Imperial Bank, and UBS, are interested in how Blockchain might improve the efficiency of their back-office settlement processes.

Smart Contracts

These Blockchain applications are contracts that execute themselves without the need for an intermediary if specific criteria provided to the computer are satisfied.

Video Games/Art

You may have heard about Crypto Kitties, a game developed on the Ethereum Blockchain. One of the game's virtual dogs was sold for more than $100,000.

Supply Chain

You can use Blockchain to monitor the provenance of precious metals and commodities in the supply chain and logistics. Walmart and IBM, for example, collaborated to develop a food traceability system based on open-source ledger technology that makes it easier to track down damaged food.

Healthcare Process Optimization

Blockchain can reduce the time it takes to pay patients' health insurance bills and store and securely communicate medical data and records.

Property

Property ownership documents may be safely saved and validated on the Blockchain, according to the real estate processing platform. Because these documents can't be tampered with, you can trust them to be correct and verify property ownership more readily.

NFT Marketplaces

These are online stores where you can buy non-fungible tokens (NFTs) and digital representations of items like paintings and apparel.

Tracking Music Royalties

Blockchain can track music streaming and compensate people who contributed to a song right away.

Emerging Blockchain Trends in 2022

Blockchain has become one of the most intriguing technology breakthroughs. In 2022, business spending on Blockchain technologies is estimated to reach $11.7 billion. In this section, we have discussed some of these trends and the factors driving them. We also provided some forecasts for how this will affect an increasing number of individuals in the coming year.

Eco-friendly Blockchain Development

Because Blockchains consume a lot of energy and produce a lot of CO_2, Tesla CEO Elon Musk decided to stop taking Bitcoin as payment for his automobiles in 2021. For this very valid reason, efforts to "greenify" Blockchain are predicted to garner much attention in 2022. There are many ways of handling this for example the adoption of carbon offsetting protocol. Many individuals, however, argue that this is simply bandaging a wound that should never have been there. Another possibility is to employ less energy-intensive Blockchain models, such as those that use "proof-of-stake" rather than "proof-of-work" methods to achieve consensus. Ethereum, the second most popular Blockchain behind Bitcoin, plans to transition to a point-of-sale (POS) mechanism in 2022. Cathy Wood, CEO of the tech-focused hedge fund Ark Invest, has advocated for a different path to a more environmentally friendly operating model. This predicts that rising energy demand will lead to increased expenditures on renewable energy generation, which will be used for various reasons, including Blockchain operation.

NFT Rise

Non-Fungible Tokens (NFTs) were the hottest topic in the Blockchain industry in 2021. Artworks like Beeple's The First 5000 Days commanded exorbitant prices, solidifying the public's understanding of unique digital tokens kept on Blockchains. It's also popular in the music industry, with artists such as Kings of Leon, Shawn Mendes, and Grimes releasing NFT-formatted works. However, like Blockchain, the concept has promise beyond its initial attention-getting applications. One example is the monster-breeding game Axie

Infinity, which allows players to "mint" their NFT creatures to dispatch into combat and now has approximately 300,000 continuous players (Fortnite, for comparison, has around 3.5 million). Similarly, Dolce & Gabbana and Nike have created NFTs for their clothing and footwear. And the Metaverse concept, championed this year by Meta, Microsoft, and Nvidia opens the door to a plethora of new NFT application cases.

Government Acceptance

In 2021, El Salvador became one of the first countries to recognize Bitcoin as a legal currency. Citizens can now use Bitcoin to purchase goods and services across the country and by businesses to pay their employees. Many analysts anticipate that many more countries will follow suit by 2022. Because of global inflation and rising remittance fees from financial intermediaries international employees use to transfer money home, Alexander Hoptner, CEO of cryptocurrency exchange BitMEX, predicts that at least five developing countries will begin to accept Bitcoin next year.

National Cryptocurrencies, in which central banks create their currency rather than accepting existing decentralized ones, will also grow in 2022. These projects typically involve digital currencies that coexist with traditional currencies, allowing users to conduct transactions and manage custody without relying on third-party service providers. Central banks also maintain control over the circulating supply, keeping the token's value pegged to the country's traditional currency. While the UK government-backed Bitcoin is unlikely to be ready for launch until 2022, other countries, including China, Singapore, Tunisia, and Ecuador, have already done so, with more to follow, including Japan, Russia, Sweden, and Estonia.

Takeaways

- A Blockchain network may be built in various ways, and it can be public, private, permissioned, or constructed by a consortium.

- The two most popular cryptocurrencies and Blockchains are Bitcoin and Ethereum.

- The Blockchain is immutable, and it automates trustworthy transactions between parties that do not need to know one other.

- Blockchain technology can be employed in industries like insurance, retail, financial services, transportation, gaming etc.

CHAPTER 1

TOKENS, COINS AND BLOCKCHAIN INVESTMENT

Crypto Token Vs Crypto Coin

Although we use the term crypto to refer to a wide range of currencies, there is a distinction between coins and tokens. Let's take a deeper look.

To better understand the crypto markets, it's easier to divide them into two categories: coins and tokens.

Coins

A coin is any cryptocurrency with its independent Blockchain, such as Bitcoin. These cryptocurrencies are built from the ground up, and the more extensive network is made with a specific aim in mind. Coin projects usually take ideas from previous technologies or other cryptocurrencies and combine them into a unique network that serves a specific purpose. Bitcoin, for example, is a censorship-resistant store of value and medium of exchange with a stable monetary policy. BTC (i.e., Bitcoins), Bitcoin's native token, is the most liquid cryptocurrency, with the most significant market cap in the Cryptocurrency industry.

Ethereum's Ether (ETH) is the native token of a smart contracts platform for writing general-purpose computer programs that run on a decentralized Blockchain and is another example of a coin. Ethereum focuses on random program data, which may range from games to social media rather than money data. Ether is used to transfer and receive money, manage assets, pay gas costs, and engage with the network's decentralized apps (dApps).

You may have also heard about Altcoins. Every coin that isn't Bitcoin is referred to as an Altcoin.

Tokens

Tokens are a particular type of smart contract that allows users to create, issue, and manage tokens derivatives of the principal Blockchain on platforms like Ethereum.

For example, Ethereum's ERC-20 token standard, which is essentially a framework for establishing tokens (other than ETH) on the Ethereum Blockchain that can be traded for one another, spurred the ICO mania of 2017. Projects would advertise or develop an Ethereum application using smart contracts, then issue a native token for usage in that application, raising cash directly from Ethereum investors.

Tokens have a distinct category in the cryptocurrency industry, serving as "utility" tokens inside an application's ecosystem for rewarding or paying fees. The MakerDAO dapp on Ethereum, for example, uses the famous ERC-20 token Dai. MakerDAO is a robust Dai-based platform that allows users to access credit instruments like lending and borrowing. ERC-20 tokens, such as Dai, can be exchanged for any other ERC-20 token or Ethereum-based standard (ERC-721), including the ETH coin. As a result, tokens like Dai exist as application-specific tokens within a coin's more extensive

Cryptocurrency/Blockchain network. Komodo (KMD), Maker (MKR), Augur (REP), 0x, and Golem are some of the other tokens available (GNT).

Because coins are created on distinct, non-standardized coding protocols, you must swap them through cryptocurrency exchanges. However, since Ethereum tokens (e.g., ERC-20) are based on established coding standards, you may trade them across inside apps with little friction.

Investing in the cryptocurrency markets can be difficult, however knowing the fundamental differences between the different cryptos can help you manage risk and make better decisions in a turbulent environment.

Hot Coins and Tokens to Invest in 2022

While you can use certain cryptocurrencies to make purchases, most people think it is a long-term investment. However, due to its volatility, it's crucial to understand what you're getting into before investing.

Hence we have summarized the top eight cryptocurrencies worth your money in 2022.

Bitcoin (BTC)

Bitcoin has the earliest history of any cryptocurrency. With a price and market size far more significant than any other crypto investment choice, it's clear to understand why it's the leader. Bitcoin is already accepted by several businesses, making it a wise investment option. Bitcoin is accepted by Visa, for example. Also, Tesla stated in

February 2021 that it had spent $1.5 billion on it, and the firm accepted it as payment for its vehicles for a period — and it may do so again if mining it becomes more ecologically friendly. In addition, central banks are starting to include Bitcoin transactions in their services.

Ethereum (ETH)

Ethereum differs from Bitcoin in that it isn't only digital money, it's also a network that allows developers to generate their currencies. While Ethereum is far behind Bitcoin in worth and TVL, it is also considerably ahead of its rivals. Although it was released years after several other cryptocurrencies, it has significantly outpaced its market position due to its unique technology. It is presently the second-largest crypto behind Bitcoin.

Binance Coin (BNB)

Binance coin took off in the first quarter of 2021, rising from around $38 on January 1 to about $683 in May, after years of relatively stable values, at least by cryptocurrency standards. It has already dropped to $382.91 as of March 8. Binance coin has proved to be one of the most solid investment alternatives due to its success. According to CoinMarketCap, Binance is the world's largest Cryptocurrency exchange.

Cardano (ADA)

For various reasons, the Cardano network has a smaller footprint, which appeals to investors. On Cardano, completing a transaction requires less energy than on a bigger network like Bitcoin, and consequently, transactions are both faster and less expensive. Last year, Cardano released a "hard fork," a software upgrade that adds new features, such as the ability to deploy smart contracts. Cardano also claims to be more versatile and safe than other cryptocurrencies. To remain ahead of hackers, it constantly enhances its growth.

Polygon (MATIC)

Polygon was developed by a group of developers that contributed significantly to the Ethereum Blockchain technology. According to CoinMarketCap, Polygon is intended for Ethereum scaling and infrastructure development. It expands Ethereum into a multi-chain system as a "layer two" solution, allowing faster transaction and verification speeds. Binance and Coinbase, two cryptocurrency exchanges, have backed Polygon. You can use its governance token, MATIC, for payment services, transaction fees, and cash settlement.

Solana (SOL)

Solana has taken the cryptocurrency industry by storm, rising from 0.01 percent of the market in 2021 to a top 10 cryptocurrency by market size by September 2021, giving Ethereum a fight for its money. According to CoinMarketCap, Solana is ranked ninth in market cap as of March 2022, with $26.4 billion. Its attractiveness stems from the network's speed, scalability, and ease with which it can be used to develop decentralized Blockchain apps.

Best Altcoins for Investment in 2022

Finding the best altcoins might be difficult for many reasons, but it's well worth it because these currencies can sometimes yield triple-digit returns.

Let's look at some of the greatest options available in 2022.

Lucky Block (LBLOCK)

When it comes to new cryptocurrencies, Lucky Block is the clear winner, as this crypto platform aims to transform the lottery sector. Lucky Block, hosted on the Binance Smart Chain, leverages Blockchain technology to improve transparency, reduce draw times, and increase an individual's likelihood of winning traditional lotteries.

The ecosystem's base is made out of LBLOCK tokens, with a part of all fees going back to holders as an incentive. Furthermore, because LBLOCK has a built-in burn rate, supply diminishes over time, increasing the price. Following a successful presale, investors can now buy LBLOCK tokens on PancakeSwap and engage in the project's Telegram channel to stay up to date on its progress.

Aave (AAVE)

Aave is widely regarded as the greatest new cryptocurrency to invest in within the DeFi market since its protocol allows users to lend and borrow money easily. Aave automatically adjusts interest rates and collateral ratios using 'liquidity pools,' controlled by smart contracts.

Shiba Inu (SHIB)

Shiba Inu is yet another new crypto to consider putting your money in 2022. SHIB exploded upon the scene in October 2021, thanks to talk from social media sites like Reddit, surging over 1000 percent in just a month. This meme coin has a similar story to Dogecoin because most of its success is founded on hype. However, because genuine use cases (such as ShibaSwap) have only recently begun, the SHIB price has room to climb through 2022.

Stellar (XLM)

Stellar is a good option if you're looking for a cryptocurrency to buy with a lot of promise. Stellar is a decentralized payment network that uses Stellar Lumens (XLM) as its native token. With the network low-cost payment structure, you can send globally, regardless of currency. This significantly improves the current financial system, making Stellar one of the best Cryptocurrencies this year.

How to Invest in Blockchain Coin

After choosing a cryptocurrency you think would be a decent investment, it's time to start buying. The first step is to create a Bitcoin exchange account. Coinbase (NASDAQ: COIN) is a prominent and user-friendly Cryptocurrency exchange in the United States. Other alternatives include Gemini and younger brokers like Robinhood (NASDAQ: HOOD) and SoFi (NASDAQ: SOFI). Just be sure that the exchange you choose supports the cryptocurrency you wish to purchase. After you've funded your account with fiat money, you can place an order to purchase cryptocurrencies.

Orders on an exchange work in the same way that stock market orders do, and the exchange will match your purchase order with a sell order simultaneously price, and the trade will be executed. After completing the transaction, the exchange will store your Bitcoin in a custodial wallet for you. The first step is to purchase cryptocurrency. You should prepare for volatility as a crypto investor. Cryptocurrency is more volatile than traditional asset classes like stocks, and price fluctuations of 10% or more in hours are not uncommon.

It would be beneficial to consider how much your portfolio you would like to allocate to a specific cryptocurrency and asset class. Due to the volatility of cryptocurrency, ensure that you have a diverse set of acceptable allocations. If your assets fall outside of specified ranges, rebalance them.

Identifying Promising Blockchain Coin

Those who had the foresight (or opportunity) to buy Bitcoin early on and then held on to it as its value soared over the previous year are now extremely wealthy. In the aftermath of Bitcoin's price surge and other digital currencies joining the market, investors are looking for the next digital currency to benefit from. But how does one go about recognizing a cryptocurrency that has the potential to grow in popularity in the future? We have summarized below the factors to consider to make a careful investment decision.

Coin Price

Keep the token's price in mind when hunting for the next star coin. For the typical investor who does not have much money to invest in the cryptocurrency business, low-cost currencies may provide the most bang for your buck. Consider a $5,000 investment: at today's rates, $5,000 might buy less than half of a Bitcoin, more than 25 Litecoins, or hundreds of coins from one or more currencies with prices less than $1 per coin. It's important not to neglect the prospect of diversifying with low-cost coins.

Adoption Possibilities

Ripple experienced substantial growth in the first half of 2018. While the price of XRP has fallen since the start of the year, it still has immense potential for adoption outside of the cryptocurrency industry. Ripple's basic technology ensures a settlement system for central banks and other financial institutions. If you can locate a cryptocurrency with an advantage over others (which is more likely to be widely embraced), this could be a wise investment.

Supply Factor

Most coins have a predetermined maximum supply. You cannot create a new coin until the limit is reached, commonly accomplished through mining. Price may grow if interest remains high while supply remains constant. Examine the total supply and current circulation before purchasing any cryptocurrency.

Price and Volume

Information on cryptocurrency trading is widely available on the internet. Those digital currencies with increasing prices and trade volume are predicted to acquire traction. Of course, there is no certainty that this trend will continue, but it is a decent way to evaluate which cryptocurrencies are now garnering the most investor attention.

Promising Blockchain stock in 2022

Many stocks are linked to Blockchain in some way. Here are some of the most popular ones traded on US markets.

Coinbase Global Inc.

Coinbase (COIN) is one of the leading exchanges in the United States. It was the first pure-play crypto trading platform to go public on Wall Street in April 2021. Coinbase generates money by allowing users to purchase and sell a wide range of digital assets.

MicroStrategy Inc.

MicroStrategy (MSTR) is an analytics software business that has amassed a sizable Bitcoin holding. Bitcoin is the first and most valued crypto, and MicroStrategy claimed to hold more than $5.2 billion in Bitcoin as of February 14, a figure close to the company's total market valuation.

NVIDIA Corp

NVIDIA (NASDAQ: NVDA) established its start as a manufacturer of computer graphics cards. However, it has recently expanded its technology usage to include Bitcoin mining. As part of the energy-intensive and possibly lucrative accounting process that allows many cryptocurrencies to operate without a central monetary authority, this procedure employs specialized equipment to solve complicated mathematical problems.

Marathon Digital Holdings Inc.

Marathon (ticker: MARA) is another corporation significantly invested in Bitcoin, providing investors with a method to have exposure to the currency without acquiring it. Marathon mines Bitcoin and invests part of its own money in the digital currency, and Marathon reported owning $387 million in Bitcoin by the end of 2021.

Block Inc.

Block (ticker: SQ) is a financial services and payment processing firm previously known as Square. Its popular Cash App product lets users invest in stocks and Bitcoin, and it has various lines of business relating to Blockchain technology and Bitcoin. At the end of 2021, Block reported it had $317 million in digital assets.

Silvergate Capital Corp.

Silvergate (ticker: SI) is a bank that provides banking and other financial services to cryptocurrency companies. It has a payment network as one of its services. The company assists clients with executing transactions.

Riot Blockchain Inc.

Riot Blockchain (ticker: RIOT) is another Bitcoin mining firm. It claims that its Rockdale, Texas, plant is the largest of its kind in North America. By the end of 2021, the corporation claimed to have a Bitcoin balance of 4,884 coins, valued at $233 million.

Advanced Micro Devices Inc.

Advanced Micro Devices (AMD) manufactures computer hardware, notably graphics processing units or GPUs. People frequently employ GPUs in cryptocurrency mining. As interest in cryptocurrency has grown, the firm has noticed greater demand for these items.

Hot Blockchain Investment Tips for 2022

When considering investing in Blockchain technology, a few things to bear in mind.

Make sure you do your homework

Many organizations claim to be active in Blockchain these days (remember Long Blockchain?), but some are more serious about the technology than others. For this reason, research into a specific company and its fundamentals are critical.

Case analysis

Building a case for the investment itself based on variables such as the chance for growth, the competitive climate, or distinguishing qualities relative to other projects is the beginning point.

Treat Blockchain like a high-risk, high-growth industry

Blockchain stocks and investments, like tech stocks, are a high-growth industry that comes with a lot of risk for investors. Because the broader value of Blockchain is still mostly unknown, it is prudent to invest just a tiny amount of your available cash in Blockchain enterprises and to diversify as much as possible in other sectors.

Watch out for new rules and regulations

It's crucial to keep up with regulators to examine individual firms, especially when so much of the Blockchain industry is still in its development stage. Government authorities and agencies might enact legislation that would severely damage Blockchain-based businesses. Understanding the regulatory background is a key indication of your investment success. With both the UK and EU devoting time to preparing for laws related to digital assets, the underlying Blockchain technology is very much on the administrations' radar as a catalyst for growth.

Concentrate on the Bitcoin connection

Yes, there are benefits to Blockchain investment over Bitcoin investing. However, because Bitcoin is still the most successful application of Blockchain technology, some experts suggest focusing on companies that primarily use it to deal with cryptocurrency. The greatest strategy to invest in firms using Blockchain technology is to look for companies utilizing Bitcoin. Square and MicroStrategy are two firms that possess Bitcoin on their balance sheets. Square, Paypal, Coinbase, Silvergate Bank, Galaxy Digital, Hive, and Voyage are two companies establishing businesses on top of Bitcoin.

Blockchain ETF Investment

With so many applications for Blockchain technology, many businesses are using it. That's why an ETF specializing in Blockchain and cryptocurrency firms is a terrific place to start when it comes to investing in the financial services sector's future.

Amplify Transformational Data Sharing ETF

Amplify Transformational Data Sharing ETF is a fantastic place to start your search for the finest Blockchain and crypto sector ETFs. It is the largest Blockchain ETF in assets (managing $1.06 billion as of January 2022). The product has a 0.71 percent cost ratio, which means that for a $1,000 investment, fees will take $7.10 from the fund's return each year. The Amplify Transformational Data Sharing ETF has 47 securities from throughout the world, with around three-quarters of them based in North America and the rest in Asia and Europe. It was started in January 2018 and has nearly doubled in value, while the majority of the gain occurred in 2020 when high-growth tech companies soared early in the year.

Coinbase Global (NASDAQ: COIN), a crypto trading platform; Nvidia (NASDAQ: NVDA), a semiconductor company that designs GPUs, the hardware required for crypto mining; and CME Group (NASDAQ: CME), a commodities exchange that supports Bitcoin (CRYPTO: BTC) and Ethereum (CRYPTO: ETH) derivatives contracts, are among the fund's top holdings.

Siren Nasdaq NexGen Economy ETF

Although the Siren Nasdaq NexGen Economy ETF is much smaller than Amplify's Blockchain ETF, it provides investors with a somewhat different perspective on the area. It comprises 64 equities, focuses on technology firms, and has less exposure to cryptocurrency holding corporations than other similar ETFs. It has a 0.68 percent expense ratio.

This ETF features a nearly 50/50 balance of domestic and overseas firms. It was introduced in January 2018 and has returned more than 70% since its debut. Coinbase, as well as older, better-known tech giants like IBM (NYSE: IBM), Accenture (NYSE: ACN), and PayPal Holdings, are among the top holdings (NASDAQ: PYPL).

First Trust Indxx Innovative Transaction & Process ETF

The First Trust Indxx Innovative Transaction & Process ETF comes next. Although First Trust is a bigger organization with a long history of developing ETFs and other financial products, this is one of its more recent releases, which began in January 2018. The fund is the most diverse Blockchain and crypto ETF, with 103 stocks. The yearly cost ratio of the First Trust Indxx Innovative Transaction & Process ETF is 0.65 percent.

More than a third of its portfolio comprises firms situated in the United States. China is the second-largest area represented, accounting for 11% of total ownership, from Europe and Asia. Some investors may prefer more overseas stock exposure, but it has driven down fund performance since early 2018. The ETF has returned less than 50% since its launch.

Micron Technology (NASDAQ: MU), AMD (NASDAQ: AMD), Nvidia, Danish shipping corporation A.P. Moeller-Maersk A/S (OTC: AMKBY), and Cognizant Technology Solutions were the top companies in the First Trust Indxx Innovative Transaction & Process ETF as of January 2022. (NASDAQ: CTSH). If you want a well-diversified portfolio with a few companies exploring Blockchain, First Trust's ETF is worth considering.

Bitwise Crypto Industry Innovators ETF

Bitwise Crypto Industry Innovators ETF is a newbie to the Blockchain ETF scene, debuting in May 2021. It has a relatively high annual expense ratio of 0.85 percent and comprises 30 equities. In a significant aspect, the Bitwise Crypto Industry Innovators ETF varies from the other funds on this list. The portfolio's equities represent a more targeted bet on the crypto industry, with many of them being Bitcoin miners and other businesses that are amassing the top cryptocurrency. Coinbase was the top holding in January 2022. MicroStrategy (NASDAQ: MSTR), a tech business and the largest Bitcoin holder, comes in second, followed by Silvergate Capital (NYSE: SI), a bank and operator of institutional crypto trading platforms. The three equities account for approximately a third of the ETF's holdings.

The Bitwise Crypto Industry Innovators ETF has usually tracked the price of Bitcoin since its inception, owing to its bias toward firms that own Bitcoin and other crypto pure-plays. The fund is now down 16%. However, with less than a year under its belt, it's too early to say how this ETF will perform. If you're looking for a way to invest in cryptocurrency without the hassles of buying it directly, this fund might be the solution.

Takeaways

- Crypto tokens are digital assets based on the Blockchain of another coin.

- Any crypto that isn't Bitcoin is referred to as altcoin. The idea of "alternative cryptocurrency" originates from the fact that they are alternatives to Bitcoin, which is the original cryptocurrency.

- Whether it's the native cryptocurrency for its Blockchain, a cryptocurrency might be a coin or a token. Crypto coins have their Blockchains, whereas crypto tokens do not.

- Stocks of companies that provide cryptocurrency-related services or are exploring other industrial uses for Blockchain technology can be used to invest in the technology.

- It is important to understand what you are getting into before investing in any coin or token.

CHAPTER 2

BLOCKCHAIN SECURITY

Basics

Blockchain security is a risk management system for a Blockchain network that uses cybersecurity frameworks, insurance services, and best practices to reduce the likelihood of attacks and fraud. Blockchain technology generates a data format that incorporates security measures. It is based on the ideas of encryption, decentralization, and consensus to ensure transaction credibility. Most Blockchains or distributed ledger technology (DLT) organize data into blocks, each containing one or more transactions. Each new block in a Blockchain connects to all previous blocks, making manipulation difficult. A consensus process verifies and agrees on all transactions within blocks, ensuring that all transactions are real and valid.

Blockchain technology supports decentralization by allowing users to participate across a decentralized network. There is no single point of failure, and one user can only change the transaction record. However, Blockchain and other systems have substantial security differences.

Blockchain and Cybersecurity Challenge

However, no technology is perfect, and Blockchain-based security is no exception. One of the protocol's intrinsic flaws is that the technology is open, allowing anybody to establish a Blockchain.

Because humans make mistakes, each Blockchain version may have vulnerabilities unique to that version. Popular chains like Bitcoin, Ethereum, and Litecoin are extensively used and thoroughly scrutinized for security flaws in the Blockchain. However, even networks based on those protocols can be subject to vulnerabilities outside the scope of the technology.

A bad actor that gains control of more than half of the devices in a Blockchain network, for example, may conceivably change transactions to transfer payments twice in a "51 percent assault." DDoS assaults, which are not confined to the Blockchain, may disrupt networks and delay transaction confirmations long enough for attackers to introduce bogus payments. There is no list of Blockchain security problems, which is an issue in and of itself, but the Cloud Security Alliance has recorded over 200 and keeps the list up to date. Many of these flaws are thought to be impossible, yet bad actors are continuously developing new ways to exploit them.

Ensuring Blockchain Security

This isn't to say that Blockchain-based businesses and services should be ignored; instead, it's important to remember certain fundamental protections. Because Bitcoin is where the money is, attackers are primarily interested in taking it. There have been few reports of attacks on non-cash applications of the technology, such as contractual, identity management, intellectual property, and other non-cash applications.

Cryptocurrency is built on open protocols, with over 4,000 distinct types available. It's riskier to experiment with lesser-known digital currency than use more recognized coins like Bitcoin. Regardless of the application, solid core standards apply to Blockchain and cyber security. In a Blockchain network, individual user accounts are the weakest link, and attackers utilize tried-and-true approaches like phishing emails to mislead users into handing over their passwords.

Too much Blockchain security, on the other side, might be a terrible thing. According to the New York Times, roughly $140 billion in Cryptocurrency appears to have been lost because the owners of the personal virtual "wallets" that store the coins have forgotten or lost their passwords.

Security Requirements of Different Blockchains

Who can participate in Blockchain networks and who has access to the data may differ. Public and private networks are frequently labeled as public or private, indicating who is allowed to join and permissioned or permissionless, signifying how users gain access to the network.

Public and Private Blockchains

Anybody can join a public Blockchain network, and participants are frequently anonymous. A public Blockchain validates transactions and establishes consensus using computers connected to the internet. Bitcoin is the most well-known example of a public Blockchain, and it creates an agreement through "Bitcoin mining." The computers on the Bitcoin network, known as "miners," attempt to solve a challenging cryptographic problem to generate proof of work and confirm the transaction. Other than public keys, there are few identification and access requirements in this type of network.

Private Blockchains rely on identities to validate membership and access credentials and thus frequently limit participation to well-known organizations. The organizations form a hidden, members-only "business network." A private Blockchain on a permissioned network achieves consensus using a process known as "selective endorsement," in which recognized users validate transactions. Members with special access and permissions can only maintain the transaction ledger. This type of network necessitates more identification and access control.

While developing a Blockchain application, it is critical to consider which type of network would best suit your company's aims. Private and permissioned networks may be tightly controlled and are desirable for compliance and regulatory reasons. However, public and permissionless networks can achieve more decentralization and dispersion.

Anyone may join and validate transactions on public Blockchains since they are open to the public. Private Blockchains are restricted, and they are mainly limited to commercial networks. A single organization or consortium controls the membership. Processors are not restricted in permissionless Blockchains. Permissioned Blockchains are only accessible to a small number of people who have been issued identities via certificates.

Cyber Attacks and Fraud

While Blockchain technology creates a tamper-proof ledger of transactions, it is not impervious to hacks or fraud. Those with malicious intent can carry out fraudulent practices on the Blockchain network and have been successful in some hacks and scams over the years. Listed below are a few examples:

Stolen Keys

The loss of roughly $73 million worth of Bitcoins from Hong Kong-based Bitfinex, one of the world's largest cryptocurrency exchanges, revealed that the currency remains a significant risk. Fraud of private keys, and personal digital signatures, is the most likely reason.

Code Exploitation

Through code exploitation, the Decentralized Autonomous Organization (DAO), a venture capital fund that operates on a decentralized Blockchain inspired by Bitcoin, was plundered of more than $60 million in ether digital currency – almost a third of its value.

Hacking Employee Computer

When Bithumb, one of the significant Ethereum and Bitcoin cryptocurrency exchanges, was recently hacked, hackers took $870,000 worth of Bitcoin and compromised the data of 30,000 users. Although an employee's PC was hacked, rather than the company's major infrastructure, the incident prompted concerns about general security.

Attacks Through Phishing

Phishing is a deceptive way of getting a user's information. Fraudsters send emails that look to be from a legitimate source to wallet key owners, and users are requested for their details via fake URLs in the emails. Getting access to a user's passwords and other private information may result in financial losses for the user and the Blockchain network.

Routing Attacks

Blockchains rely on massive real-time data transfers, and hackers can steal data as it is delivered to internet service providers. Because Blockchain participants cannot detect the threat posed by a routing attack, everything looks normal. On the other side, fraudsters have stolen private data or currency behind the scenes.

Sybil Attack

Hackers create and use several fake network identities in a Sybil attack to flood the network and destroy the system. Sybil is a made-up character with multiple personality disorder.

51% Attacks

Mining requires tremendous processing power, especially for large-scale public Blockchains. Nevertheless, if a miner or group of miners can pool enough resources, they may be able to control more than half of the mining power on a Blockchain network. Controlling the ledger and having the ability to modify it entails possessing more than half of the power. However, private Blockchains are not vulnerable to 51% attacks.

Blockchain Security Tips and Practices

Consider the following critical questions while developing a Blockchain solution:

What is the governance model for members of participating organizations?

What information will be collected in each block?

What regulatory standards must be satisfied, and how can they be accomplished?

How are identity-related details managed? Is the data in block payloads encrypted?

How are keys kept track of and revoked?

What is the Blockchain participants' disaster recovery plan?

What is the minimum level of security that Blockchain clients must have to participate?

What is the reasoning behind resolving block collisions on the Blockchain?

Below are some commonly used practices and tips to secure the Blockchain network.

- When developing a private Blockchain, ensure that it runs on a secure, dependable infrastructure. Bad technology choices for company goals and operations can result in data security issues due to their flaws.

- Think about the threats to your business and governance. Business risks include financial penalties, reputational problems, and compliance hazards. Due to the decentralized nature of Blockchain network, governance difficulties arise, necessitating strict controls on decision criteria, governing protocols, identity and access management.

- Understanding and managing Blockchain network risks are critical for Blockchain security. A Blockchain security model is being developed to provide security to these controls. Make a Blockchain security model ensure that all required measures are in place to make your Blockchain solutions secure.

- Administrators must build a risk model to manage all business, governance, technological, and process concerns to execute a Blockchain solution security model. Next, they must assess the risks associated with the Blockchain solution and develop a threat model. Then, depending on the three categories below, administrators must create the security measures that will reduce the risks and threats:

Implement Blockchain-specific security mechanisms.

Use standard security measures.

Ensure that firm controls are in place for Blockchain.

Blockchain Penetration Testing

Penetration testing on a Blockchain-based solution or application is a security evaluation procedure carried out by ethical hackers or security professionals to determine the solution's or application's security strength. The main goal of Blockchain penetration testing is to find vulnerabilities and security flaws in the system and misconfiguration problems. Organizations may get insight into their entire Blockchain security posture and remedy possible holes in their Blockchain-based systems or apps by doing Blockchain penetration testing.

Blockchain Security Case Studies

Here are a few instances of how companies deal with Blockchain security.

Mobilecoin

This cryptocurrency firm located in California is working on a secure, user-friendly cryptocurrency for businesses that can't afford to adopt ledger security measures on their own. Mobilecoin's cryptocurrency eliminates the need for third-party transaction suppliers by encrypting all transaction data on both ends. Facebook Messenger, WhatsApp, and Signal are all supported by the app.

Coinbase

Coinbase is another cryptocurrency firm situated in California. Coinbase is a cryptocurrency exchange where you can buy and sell digital money, and Coinbase handles wallets and passwords in a secure database solely on encryption. To protect the safety of Bitcoin, employees must go through a thorough background check.

J.P. Morgan

J.P. Morgan is one of the prominent and largest financial organizations in the United States. It has created Quorum, an enterprise-focused version of Ethereum that uses Blockchain technology to process private transactions. J.P. Morgan's Quorum network employs smart contracts to provide visible yet cryptographically secure transactions.

Lockheed Martin

Lockheed is a defense contractor located in the United States. It is the first of its kind to incorporate Blockchain security. Lockheed Martin and Guardtime Federal collaborate to implement Blockchain cybersecurity protocols in engineering systems, software development, and supply chain risk management. The objective of Lockheed Martin is to employ Blockchain to secure every step of the weapon development process.

Cisco

This Silicon Valley behemoth believes that Blockchain is great for the Internet of Things (IoT) because the built-in ledger technology eliminates single points of failure and encrypts essential personal data. This concept is crucial since the Internet of Things has been continuously increasing. If Blockchain technology becomes the dominant IoT network, its visibility and utilization will increase. Of course, having a major IoT player on your side can't hurt!

Hashed Health

This healthcare innovation startup in Tennessee aims to assist the healthcare industry in using Blockchain technology. Hashed Collective, Hashed Enterprise, and Hashed Labs are the three entities that make up the company, and each focuses on a different part of the Blockchain. Many hospitals and healthcare firms have joined Hashed Health to create secure digital Blockchain networks devoted to patient information exchange and secure internal communication channels.

Top Blockchain Security Startups in 2022

Business models vary throughout time, sometimes due to market shifts and technological advancements, leading to the birth of new and exciting trends. There are 119 Blockchain Security companies in the world, and here is a list of the five most promising ones:

Chainalysis

Chainalaysis offer cryptocurrency investigation, transaction, and monitoring solutions. It provides various services for businesses, financial institutions, and government agencies, including Blockchain-based payment fraud prevention and compliance management solutions, digital identity and malicious activity monitoring solutions, transaction-based risk scoring solutions, due diligence, and investigation tools.

Overview of the company

Year of Inception 2014

Funding 367 million dollars

Location New York (United States)

Investors Their investors include GIC, Marc Benioff, Sequoia Capital, and 29 others.

Elliptic

For crypto businesses, elliptic transaction monitoring and fraud prevention solutions are available. It provides solutions for Blockchain analytics, crypto compliance, financial crime risk management, and more for crypto enterprises. It also provides services like an elliptic discovery for finding and analyzing crypto-asset exposure, a lens for inspecting crypto wallets, and a navigator for managing crypto risk.

Overview of the company

Year of Inception 2014

Funding 104 million dollars

Location London (United Kingdom)

Investors SoftBank Vision Fund, Seedcamp, Tech Nation, and 16 other investors are among those who have invested in Elliptic.

Simplex

Simplex provides organizations with AI-based crypto payment and fraud prevention solutions. It allows businesses to accept cryptocurrency payments for various goods and services. It also has a worldwide fiat onramp for debit and credit card transactions. It will enable companies to accept cryptocurrency payments for multiple goods and services. Escrow services for numerous fiat-crypto transactions are also available.

Overview of the company

Year of Inception 2014

Funding 19 million dollars

Location Ramat Gan (Israel)

Investors FundersClub, F2 Capital, Korea Investment Partners, and nine other investors participated in the round.

Fireblocks

Fireblocks is a cryptocurrency financial services company. It provides services such as cryptocurrency wallets, cryptocurrency exchange platforms, cryptocurrency trading platforms, asset tokenization, etc. It also includes solutions for automated crypto transaction governance and oversight.

Overview of the company

Year of Inception 2018

Location Tel Aviv (Israel), New York City (United States)

Funding 489 million dollars

Investors Marius Nacht, Swisscom, Swisscom, and 24 Other Investors

Casa

Casa is a private key management software built on the blockchain. A multi-signature strategy protects investments from fraud, natural catastrophes, accidents, etc. A key recovery service is also available.

Overview of the company

Year of Inception 2016

Location New York City (United States)

Funding 10 million dollars

Investors Castle Island Ventures, Fabric Ventures, Precursor Ventures, and ten other investors are among those who have invested.

Key Takeaways

- Blockchain security is a risk management system for a Blockchain network that employs cybersecurity frameworks, insurance services, and best practices to reduce the risk of attacks and fraud.

- Networks are usually classified as public or private, based on who is permitted to join and whether they are permissioned or not. Permissioned or permissionless defines how users obtain access to the network.

- Anyone may join and validate transactions on public Blockchains since they are open to the public.

- Private Blockchains are exclusive to business networks and are frequently restricted. A single organization or consortium controls the membership.

- Processors are not restricted in permissionless Blockchains.

- Permissioned Blockchains are only accessible to a restricted number of users who have been issued identities via certificates.

- Blockchain technology creates a tamper-proof ledger of transactions but it is not impervious to hacks or fraud. You need to make sure you understand how these scams work and how to prevent them.

CHAPTER 3

DECENTRALIZED (DISTRIBUTED) LEDGERS

Meaning of Distributed Ledger

Distributed ledgers are databases that are shared across a network and dispersed across several sites. A ledger is a collection of financial accounts that are spread out and handled internationally in this situation. As a result, several people in various places and institutions hold and restructure dispersed ledgers. Participants at each network node can review distributed ledgers and acquire an identical copy of the records shared across the network. The modifications are reproduced and copied to the participants whenever the ledger is modified or added. The database is synced to ensure that it is correct. Bitcoin and distributed ledgers both employ the same technology.

Mechanism of Distributed Ledger

Individuals known as nodes hold, restructure, and control distributed ledgers. Each node creates the database on its own. Every transaction on the network is evaluated, and each node creates a conclusion about the database's evolution. Voting is done on the database modifications that have been finalized based on the transaction. All nodes vote and the new transaction is allowed on the database if at least 51 percent of them agree. Following that, the nodes update the database versions so

49

that all devices or nodes are on the same version. The new transaction is recorded in a Blockchain block.

Miners are the nodes in a Proof-of-Work Blockchain. A miner is rewarded for successfully inserting a new transaction into a block. It needs a computer with devoted power 24 hours a day, seven days a week. Miners are in charge of computing the cryptographic hash for new blocks. The reward is given to the miner who correctly finds the hash first. Miners that devote more processing power to finding the hash will have a better chance of succeeding. However, finding subsequent hash scales becomes more complicated when more blocks are generated.

Benefits of Distributed Ledgers
Extremely clear, safe, tamper-proof, and unchangeable

The entries in distributed ledgers take place in the database without the intervention of a third party. No one else can change records once recorded into distributed ledgers. As a result, the records cannot be changed until the ledgers are disseminated.

There is no need for a third party

Although it is not always required to manage distributed ledgers without the help of a third party, in some circumstances, it may save a lot of money and time. Sensors may immediately write findings to the Blockchain in the supply chain industry, eliminating the need for a third party. It helps you save a lot of money, time, and effort.

Decentralized by nature

The inherently decentralized nature of distributed ledgers offers another degree of protection. It is difficult to attack the database since it is distributed globally.

It is very Transparent.

Transparency is a crucial feature of distributed ledgers. They make it possible to view all of the information that has been stored in a free and straightforward manner, and it offers several sectors an excellent level of openness.

Key Takeaways

- Distributed ledgers are databases that are shared across a network and accessible from several places.

- Individuals known as nodes are in charge of holding, reorganizing, and controlling them. Distributed ledgers eliminate the requirement for a third party.

- Because distributed ledgers are naturally decentralized and give a high level of transparency, they are regarded as very secure.

CHAPTER 4

SMART CONTRACTS

Basics of Smart Contract

Smart contracts are simply programs that run when specific criteria are met and are stored on a Blockchain. They are typically used to automate the implementation of a contract so that all parties can be confident of the outcome without the need for intermediaries. They can also manage a workflow, commencing the next phase when specific conditions are met.

Simple "if/when...then..." lines are placed into Blockchain code to make smart contracts work. When certain conditions are met and approved, the actions are carried out by a network of computers. These tasks could include transferring funds to the appropriate parties, registering a vehicle, sending alerts, or issuing a ticket. The Blockchain is updated once the transaction is completed. The update shows that the transaction is irreversible and that the results are only accessible to those granted access.

A smart contract can include as many parameters as necessary to persuade the parties that the work will be completed appropriately. To determine the conditions, participants must agree on how transactions and associated data are represented on the Blockchain, decide on the "if/when...then..." rules that govern those transactions, explore all potential exceptions, and design a structure for resolving disputes. A developer can then code the smart contract; however, companies that use Blockchain for business increasingly provide templates, web interfaces, and other online tools to make Smart Contract production easier.

Benefits of Smart Contracts
Accuracy, speed, and efficiency

When a condition is met, the contract is immediately executed. Because smart contracts are digital and automated, there is no paperwork to deal with, and no time is lost fixing errors that may occur when filling out paperwork by hand.

Transparency and trust

There is no need to be concerned about information being tampered with for personal advantage because no third party is involved, and encrypted transaction logs are distributed among participants.

Safety

Because Blockchain transaction records are encrypted, they are difficult to hack. Furthermore, because each record on a distributed ledger is linked to the previous and subsequent entries, hackers would have to change the entire chain to change a single record.

Savings

Smart contracts remove the need for intermediaries to perform transactions and the time delays and costs that come with them.

Smart Contract Applications and Use Cases in 2022

Let's look at some smart contract use cases to understand better how they are helpful in Blockchain development.

Cryptographic Tokens

Tokens, often known as cryptographic tokens or just tokens, are digital assets stored on a Blockchain. Tokens symbolize a platform's right to use, a financial investment, or a piece of digital real estate. If you want to enjoy Netflix2.0's streaming services, you'll need to buy a Netflix token, which you'll need to use once a month. A token represents a portion of a bond, with periodical interest payments and repayment at the maturity date.

The Ethereum request for comment (ERC-20) standard, initially suggested by Fabian Vogelsteller, is used to issue most tokens on the Ethereum network. A smart contract that determines the total supply and the rules for token transfers, among other things, is used to create a token. The ERC-20 token standard is a smart contract template that makes it simple to create tokens and integrate them with various wallets and exchanges. Here is an easy-to-follow instruction for you to look at the process of issuing a token or even test it out for yourself.

Payment Channels

Payment channels are another use case that isn't commonly linked with smart contracts. In the broadest sense, they allow interactions off-chain to be just as trustworthy as that on-chain. The lightning network on Bitcoin is undoubtedly the most popular payment channel network.

Elimination of Middlemen

Smart contracts promise to eliminate the need for intermediaries such as attorneys and notaries, lowering business costs. Most significantly, they save time for participants by eliminating the need for intermediaries. This can manifest itself in a variety of ways. Consider a sports club's ticketing system. It just takes one open-source version of a ticketing platform to render numerous ticketing businesses obsolete, rather than involving a third party that collects fees.

Decentralized Applications (dApps)

Decentralized apps, or dApps, are frequently addressed in the context of smart contracts. A decentralized application (dApp) might be anything from a decentralized exchange to an auctioning platform or even a game. A dApp, like any other program, lets its users accomplish a set of operations, actions, or activities. Most traditional apps connect with their many components through APIs (application programming interfaces), such as social network integrations, underlying databases, or microservices.

A dApp communicates with its underlying Blockchain and non-blockchain components via one or more smart contracts. Smart contracts detect incoming payments from users, issue payments to those users, operate as escrow, or initiate an action depending on data given by the users.

Blockchain and Smart Contract Implementation

Smart Contracts based on Ethereum produce digital tokens for transaction purposes. You may create a marketable computerized token by designing and issuing your own digital money. A standard coin API is used to create the tokens. In the case of Ethereum, there are ERC 2.0 standardizations that allow the contract to access any wallet for exchange immediately. As a result, you will create a fixed-supply tradable token. The platform takes on the role of a central bank, issuing digital currency.

Assume you want to create a firm that requires capital. However, who would lend money to someone they don't know or trust? Smart contracts have a significant role. You may use Ethereum to create a smart contract that will retain a contributor's cash until a deadline or a goal is accomplished. The monies are either disbursed to the contract owners or returned to the contributors based on the outcome. The administration methods of the centralized crowdfunding system are riddled with flaws. A DAO (Decentralized Autonomous Organization) is used for crowdfunding to combat this. The contract specifies the terms and circumstances, and each person who participates in crowdfunding receives a token. On the Blockchain, each contribution is recorded.

Limitation of Smart Contract

As crucial as the smart contract is to the blockchain operation, it also suffers some limitation. Below are a few notable of them.

- Smart contracts can't get information about "real-world" events since they can't make HTTP requests. This is on purpose.
- Using third-party data might endanger consensus, which is necessary for security and decentralization.

Future of Smart Contracts

Smart requirements-powered contracts are unquestionably the way for relatively simple contracts that can be prepared and executed once pre-conditions are satisfied, such as in residential conveyancing, where completion payments are delivered as soon as documents are signed. Smart contract platforms will save businesses worldwide time and money while also altering how they engage with their consumers and in the supply chain. Consequently, people and key decision-makers will be freed from dealing with monotonous administration and red tape, focusing on their day jobs. The reason for this is that the smart contract takes up the slack.

Many banks and insurance companies are already using smart contracts in their regular operations. Consequently, smart contracts are nowhere and are being tested in real-world circumstances, and it won't be long until they're ingrained in our daily lives. Regardless of the previous reasoning, it will be long before a smart contract regulates everything.

Smart Contract Platforms for Investing in 2022

Stellar

Stellar is a decentralized network for holding and moving money that allows users to generate, send, and exchange digital representations of any currency, including dollars, pesos, and Bitcoin. It's built so that all of the world's financial systems may communicate through a single network, making it a good investment option.

Symbol

The NEM Group describes Symbol as a reliable, secure value exchange network for businesses. Symbol reduces corporate friction by increasing data flow and innovation, boosting asset creation, exchange, and protection.

SmartChain

SmartChain provides the infrastructure that allows organizations to integrate Blockchain into their operations. Its goal is to give users a drag-and-drop interface to let them build smart contracts faster and with less code.

TRON

TRON is a Blockchain-based decentralized platform that creates a free, worldwide digital content entertainment system using distributed storage technology and makes digital content sharing cost-effective and straightforward.

Stratis

Stratis is a business-grade development platform specializing in native C# and NET Blockchain applications. The heart of Stratis is an open-source proprietary Blockchain that offers unprecedented network performance and scalability while maintaining accessibility and flexibility.

Key Takeaways

- Smart contracts are digital contracts that are automatically executed if preset terms and circumstances are satisfied and are maintained on a Blockchain.

- Blockchain transaction records are encrypted, making them extremely difficult to hack.

- There are a variety of smart contract implementations that can automate the world and make it a better place to live.

- Smart contract Blockchains offer several advantages, including increased speed, efficiency, accuracy, trust, transparency, security, and cost savings.

CHAPTER 5

DECENTRALIZED FINANCE (DeFi)

Basics

The move from old, centralized financial institutions to peer-to-peer financing is facilitated by decentralized technology built on the Ethereum Blockchain, known as decentralized finance or DeFi. DeFi's ecosystem has created a broad network of interconnected protocols and financial products, ranging from lending and borrowing platforms to stable coins and tokenized BTC. Decentralized finance has emerged as the most active industry in the Blockchain realm, with over $13 billion in wealth locked in Ethereum smart contracts and many use cases for people, developers, and institutions. Unlike our traditional financial system, which is powered by code that runs on the Ethereum Blockchain's decentralized infrastructure and is managed by central authorities, institutions, and intermediaries, decentralized finance is powered by code that runs on the Ethereum Blockchain's decentralized infrastructure. DeFi developers may establish financial protocols and platforms that execute as designed and are accessible to anybody with an internet connection by deploying immutable smart contracts on Ethereum.

Benefits of Decentralized Finance

Decentralized finance uses the Ethereum Blockchain's main concepts to improve financial security and transparency, open liquidity and development potential, and promote a unified and uniform economic system.

Programmability.

Smart contracts are highly programmable contracts that automate execution and enable the development of innovative financial instruments and digital assets. Smart contracts are highly programmable contracts that automate execution and enable the development of innovative financial instruments and digital assets.

Immutability

Immutability is a term used to describe the ability to change one's mind. Data coordination across a Blockchain's decentralized technology is tamper-proof, improving security and auditability.

Interoperability

Interoperability is a term used to describe the capacity of two or more systems to communicate. Because of Ethereum's composable software architecture, DeFi protocols and apps are designed to integrate and complement one another. Developers and product teams can construct interfaces and connect third-party apps to DeFi by building on top of existing protocols. As a result, DeFi protocols are often known as "money legos."

Transparency

Every transaction on the Ethereum public Blockchain is broadcast to and confirmed by other network members (note: Ethereum addresses are pseudo-anonymous encrypted keys). This level of transaction data transparency allows for comprehensive data analysis and ensures that network activity is accessible to all users. Ethereum and the DeFi protocols that run on it are built with open source code that everyone can see, audit, and modify.

Permissionless

Unlike traditional finance, DeFi is characterized by open, permissionless access: anybody with a crypto wallet and an Internet connection may use DeFi applications built on Ethereum, regardless of location or money.

Self-Custody

DeFi market participants permanently preserve custody of their assets and control of their data by interacting with permissionless financial applications and protocols utilizing Web3 wallets like MetaMask.

DeFi Use Cases

Decentralized financial protocols have opened up a world of new economic activity and opportunities for people all around the globe, from DAOs to synthetic assets. DeFi is much more than an emerging ecosystem of projects, as seen by the extensive list of use cases below. Instead, it's a massive and well-coordinated effort to create an alternative financial system on Ethereum that can compete with centralized services regarding accessibility, resilience, and transparency.

Asset Management

You are the custodian of your crypto assets using DeFi protocols. Crypto wallets like MetaMask, Gnosis Safe, and Argent make it safe and straightforward to conduct anything from buying, trading, and transferring cryptocurrency to earning income on your digital assets. You control your data in the DeFi world: MetaMask, for example, keeps your seed phrase, passwords, and private keys locally on your device in an encrypted format so that only you have access to your accounts and data.

When it comes to allocating cash into DeFi, the game changes for firms with higher institutional-grade needs. Wallets like MetaMask Institutional make crypto-economic research, pre-and post-trade compliance, optimal trade execution, reporting, and crypto custody easier for these businesses.

Compliance and KYT

Know-your-customer (KYC) principles are used in conventional finance to ensure anti-money laundering. (AML) and counter-terrorist financing (CFT) compliance. Ethereum's decentralized architecture allows for next-generation compliance analysis based on the behavior of participating addresses rather than participant identities in the DeFi space. This know-your-transaction (KYT) service, such as those offered by MetaMask Institutional, assist in the real-time assessment of risk and the prevention of fraud and financial crimes.

DAOs (Decentralized Autonomous Organizations)

A DAO is a decentralized autonomous organization that cooperates according to transparent rules stored on the Ethereum Blockchain, obviating the necessity for a centralized administrative institution. Maker and Compound, two popular DeFi protocols, have developed DAOs to collect funds, run financial operations, and decentralize governance to the community.

Analytics and Data

DeFi protocols benefit data discovery, analysis, and decision-making around financial possibilities and risk management due to their extraordinary openness surrounding transaction data and network activities. DeFi Pulse is one of several tools and dashboards that enable customers to track the value locked in DeFi protocols, measure platform risk, and compare yield and liquidity.

Derivatives

Smart contracts based on Ethereum allow for the construction of tokenized derivatives whose value is generated from the performance of an underlying asset and where counterparty agreements are hardcoded in code. DeFi derivatives can represent real-world assets and cryptocurrencies, such as fiat currencies, bonds, and commodities.

Developer and Infrastructure Tooling

Composability is one of the key design concepts of DeFi protocols, which means that various system components can readily connect and communicate. Composable code has produced a significant network effect in which the community continues to build upon what others have developed, as seen by the extensive range of integrated DeFi apps. Many people compare DeFi development to constructing with legos, earning the moniker "money legos." Ethereum developers and product teams can now design and launch DeFi protocols with the full-stack tooling and security integrations they require, thanks to Truffle's Smart Contract libraries, Infura's API suite, and Diligence's security tools.

DEXs

DEXs are cryptocurrency exchanges that operate without a central authority, enabling users to transact peer-to-peer while maintaining control over their cash. Because crypto-assets are never in possession of the exchange, DEXs lessen the danger of price manipulation, hacking, and theft. DEXs also provide token projects with liquidity that rivals centralized exchanges while avoiding listing costs. Projects would spend millions of dollars to get a token listed on a controlled exchange just a few years ago.

Some exchanges leverage decentralization, with centralized servers hosting order books and other functions but not holding users' private keys. Air Swap, Liquality, Mesa, Oasis, and Uniswap are some of the most popular DEXs in the DeFi sector. MetaMask Swaps, for example, optimizes trading experiences by giving DeFi customers unique knowledge, allowing them to determine the best price quotation and excellent gas prices for the provided quote and the lowest failure rates.

Gaming

DeFi's modularity has enabled product developers to integrate DeFi protocols directly into platforms across various industries. Because of their built-in economies and creative incentive structures, Ethereum-based games have become a prominent use case for decentralized finance. For example, PoolTogether is a no-loss audited saving lottery that allows users to buy digital tickets by depositing the DAI stablecoin, which is then pooled and loaned to the Compound money market protocol to earn interest.

Best DeFi Projects

The Terra (LUNA)

The Terra Blockchain technology creates stable price payment systems for various currencies by using fiat-pegged stablecoins. It provides USD, South Korean Won, Mongolian Tugrik, and the International Monetary Fund's Special Drawing Rights basket of currencies as stablecoins.

LUNA is Terra's native token. The token is used to keep the price of the protocol's stablecoins stable and submit and vote on governance ideas. Terra has also secured collaborations with several payment systems, including Chai (a mobile payment app located in South Korea). Terra is now one of the most rapidly expanding crypto ecosystems, with over 100 projects spanning DeFi, Web3, and NFTs (Non-Fungible Tokens).

DAI (DAI)

DAI is a stablecoin based on Ethereum that was established and is administered by the Maker Platform and MakerDAO. DAI is distinct from other popular stablecoins in that it is entirely decentralized and is used by hundreds of dapps and DeFi projects. The DAI stablecoin was formerly exclusively collateralized with Ethereum, but it is now multi-collateralized.

The majority of decentralized currencies underperformed. However, DAI has risen in popularity and use cases by maintaining a stable price near $1. The Decentralized Autonomous Organization supports the stablecoin overcollateralized to keep the pegging steady. Anyone that has collateral may manufacture DAI tokens. Hence there is no need for a centralized entity to supervise the process.

Chainlink (LINK)

Many crypto Dapps require oracles to interface with various types of data. Chainlink is the current leader in oracles. Through a network of oracles and Smart Contracts, Chainlink provides a decentralized data set that bridges the gap between real-world data and blockchain applications. Since its inception in 2019, Chainlink has grown at a breakneck pace, now delivering over 75 price feeds to over 300 Smart Contracts and decentralized apps.

It's worth noting that Chainlink has grown and matured to the point where it now awards funds to crypto projects judged beneficial to the ecosystem. Chainlink has a huge influence in the DeFi domain by assisting other projects with oracles to assure their operation. Synthetic, AAVE, and KyberSwap are a few famous projects that use Chainlink oracles.

Avalanche (AVAX)

Avalanche is a platform for building decentralized finance apps, financial assets, and other services using interoperable smart contracts. The platform supports the Ethereum virtual machine, application-specific sharding, network-level programmability, and NFTs. Avalanche is a network that employs a proof-of-stake consensus mechanism to allow users to trade and launch decentralized assets with sub-second transaction confirmations.

Uniswap (UNI)

Uniswap is well recognized as the current decentralized cryptocurrency exchange market leader. Hayden Adams established it in 2017 as a decentralized exchange based on the Ethereum network. The trading system was created as an on-chain automated market maker (AMM) that can set a cryptocurrency's price based on the ratio of two coins in a pool.

Different DeFi tokens, as well as Liquidity Provider tokens, can be exchanged and traded on Uniswap. Even if an ERC20 token isn't listed, you can still construct a pair and exchange it for another cryptocurrency if you identify the smart contract's address. Users can also supply liquidity in current pools or build new pools to provide for and exchange.

Hot DeFi Coin in 2022

To select the best DeFi coins for your investment portfolio, consider the following criteria:

- Current market capitalization
- Goals and objectives set in the past, as well as a road plan for the future
- Potential for expansion
- The cost of a token

- Exchanges that have the token listed

When assessing your alternatives, keep in mind that the most discounted cryptos frequently have the most potential for exponential growth in the future.

Considering these key ideas, here is a list of the best DeFi coins for 2022.

Lucky Block

In general, Lucky Block appears as the best DeFi coin to invest in currently. The project, which began at the end of 2021, is nearing completion with a new lottery gaming platform launch. The Lucky Block lottery ecosystem is distinct from traditional operators in that all game outcomes are decentralized. As a result, unlike many other types of gambling, lotteries are not managed by government-sponsored institutions. This demonstrates the opportunity that surrounds this coin. Lucky Block token first held a pre-sale in January 2022, raising $5 million in crypto-equivalent. Lucky Block token became public on Pancakeswap near the end of the month, and it has since been one of the finest digital assets of the year.

To demonstrate this argument, during its inaugural pre-sale campaign, Lucky Block was priced at merely $0.00015. Since then, the project has reached highs of $0.00961 per token, according to Coin Market Cap. As a result, in just over a month of trading, this represents gains of over 6,000 percent. Finally, by purchasing Lucky Block now, you can still get in on the ground floor of this promising project.

Uniswap

Uniswap is the next coin on the list of finest DeFi coins to watch in 2022. It houses a novel exchange platform that allows traders to swap tokens on a peer-to-peer basis. This project exemplifies the actual concept of decentralized finance. To put it another way, Uniswap eliminates the need for a centralized intermediary when buying and selling crypto assets.

In contrast to the industry standard controlled by giant centralized crypto exchanges like Binance, FTX, and Coinbase, this is a welcome shift. All of which acts as a middleman between buyers and sellers, raking in large profits. The exchange does not use traditional order books to match market participants in the case of Uniswap. Instead, an automated market maker – or AMM – model resides on the platform. Uniswap's AMM, in its most basic version, will establish token values depending on a range of criteria, including volume, demand, and market capitalization. This makes it possible to trade Bitcoins in a decentralized and hassle-free manner.

The project's native DeFi token, UNI, is a top-25 digital asset in market value. You would have spent around $7 when the coin was initially released on public markets in 2020. UNI has reached highs of about $17 year-to-date in 2022, and this is an increase of more than 140 percent. Investors expect UNI to return to the $40+ range it reached in 2021.

Terra

There's no doubting that the global cryptocurrency markets, particularly those for DeFi coins, have been overwhelmingly pessimistic heading into 2022. With that considered, the value of Terra – which continues to perform exceptionally well – looks to be unstoppable. Terra is a decentralized finance project that specializes in algorithmic stablecoins for those who are unfamiliar, and LUNA is the native token.

Unlike other stablecoins on the market, Terra isn't limited to big fiat currencies like the US dollar or the euro. The Terra protocol covers various national currencies, including the South Korean won, Japanese yen, and Chinese yuan. In truth, Terra is a supporter of the SDR (Special Drawing Rights), the International Monetary Fund's currency. Terra was valued at just $1.30 per token when it was first listed on public exchanges in 2019 — according to CoinMarketCap. In early 2022, the identical DeFi coin will be worth more than $90.

Decentraland

In 2022, what is the finest Metaverse coin? The Metaverse is predicted to grow in popularity in the future, with companies like Meta announcing their interest in the space. If you want to get in on the ground floor of this developing concept, you may buy MANA tokens, Decentraland's original digital asset.

Decentraland is a project built on top of the Ethereum Blockchain that provides everyone with access to a virtual game environment. Users may buy virtual land and then create digital real estate on Decentraland, one of the platform's unique aspects. The open marketplace may then be used to sell this real estate and other in-game commodities. For many reasons, this business model has already demonstrated its viability. To begin with, certain real estate plots sold through the Decentralized platform have raised more than a million dollars.

Second, the MANA token, which serves as the native currency for all Decentraland platform purchases and sales, is currently a multibillion-dollar coin. MANA was just worth $0.025 in terms of performance in 2018. The crypto asset reached highs of around $6 in mid-2021. As a result, this is a substantial increase of approximately 24,000 percent, making it a fantastic investment option.

Yearn. Finance

Services Yearn. Finance is the next project on the list of the finest DeFi coins for 2022 to consider. This project specializes in decentralized financial services, focusing on peer-to-peer loans. Yearn. Finance acts as a conduit between borrowers and lenders, eliminating the need for a centralized middleman.

This is made possible through smart contract technology, which allows regular people to utilize Yearn.Finance to borrow money without having to go through a credit check. Investors that want to earn a return on their idle Bitcoin assets support these loans. Investors will benefit from this by making a high rate of return. Yearn. Finance also allows investors to provide liquidity for trading pairs, resulting in an APY exceeding what traditional banks and financial institutions can offer. You may invest in the Yearn. Finance project by acquiring the Yearn. Finance DeFi coin - YFI.

According to CoinMarketCap, YFI was initially listed on public exchanges in July 2020 for $907. Since then, the YFI coin has risen to almost $93,000 in value. This equates to profits of more than 10,000 percent. Another significant advantage of the DeFi coin is that the entire quantity of this digital asset is highly restricted, at just over 36,000 tokens.

Takeaways

- The move from traditional, centralized financial systems to peer-to-peer financing facilitated by decentralized technology built on the Ethereum Blockchain is called decentralized finance.

- Decentralized finance uses the Ethereum Blockchain's main concepts to improve financial security and transparency, open liquidity and development potential, and promote a unified and uniform economic system.

- Decentralized financial protocols have opened up a world of new economic activity and opportunities for people worldwide, from DAOs to synthetic assets and much more.

Dear Reader,

As independent authors it's often difficult to gather reviews compared with much bigger publishers.

Therefore, please leave a review on the platform where you bought this book.

Many thanks,

Author Team

CHAPTER 6

BLOCKCHAIN WALLETS

Meaning of Blockchain Wallet

A Blockchain wallet is a form of cryptocurrency wallet that allows users to handle several cryptocurrencies, including Bitcoin and Ethereum. A Blockchain wallet simplifies the exchange of money. Transactions are secure because they are cryptographically signed. The wallet can be accessed from any internet device, including handheld devices, and the user's identity and privacy are safeguarded. As a result, a Blockchain wallet possesses all the properties required for safe and secure financial transactions and swaps between participants.

Blockchain Wallet Mechanism

Let's start with defining private and public keys and how they relate to a Blockchain wallet. When you establish a Blockchain wallet, you will be given a private key and a public key linked to your wallet. As an example, consider email, and you offer someone your email address if you wish to get an email from them. However, giving up your email address does not imply that others will be allowed to send emails from your account. To do so, someone would need to have your email account's password. In Blockchain wallets, a public key and a private key are used in the same way. A public key is similar to an email address because it can be shared with anybody. When you create your wallet, a public key is generated that you can share with anyone to take cash.

The private key is a highly guarded secret that, like your password, should not be hacked and should not be disclosed to anybody. You spend your money with the help of this private key. If someone acquires access to the private key, there is a good possibility that your account will be hacked, and all of your Bitcoin deposits will be lost.

Blockchain Wallet Features

Now that you understand how Blockchain wallets work, it's critical to understand their features. The following are some of the essential features of Blockchain wallets:

- It's simple to use, and it works simply like any other piece of software or wallet you use daily.
- Extremely safe. It's simply a matter of keeping your private key safe.
- It allows for cross-border transactions in real-time. These are also barrier-free, as there are no intermediaries.
- Transaction costs are low compared to traditional banks, and the price of transferring funds is significantly lower.
- It allows for the exchange of several cryptocurrencies, making currency conversions simple.

Blockchain Wallet Types

Hot and cold wallets are the two types of Blockchain wallets based on private keys. Hot wallets are user-friendly and similar to a wallet we use for everyday transactions. Cold wallets are comparable to vaults in that they store cryptocurrency securely. Let's go over some more details to understand these two types of wallet.

Hot Wallets and Cold Wallets

Hot wallets are online wallets that allow you to send and receive coins instantly. They may be found on the internet. Coinbase and Blockchain.info are two examples. Cold wallets are digital offline wallets that sign transactions offline before disclosing them online. They are not kept in the cloud on the internet; instead, they are kept offline for maximum protection. Trezor and Ledger are two examples of cold wallets. Private keys are saved in the cloud with hot wallets for speedier transfers. Private keys are held in cold wallets on separate hardware that is not linked to the internet or the cloud or on a paper document. Hot wallets are accessible online 24 hours a day, seven days a week, and maybe accessed through a desktop or mobile device. However, there is a danger of unrecoverable loss if they are hacked. The manner of transactions in cold wallets helps safeguard the wallet from illegal access (hacking and other online vulnerabilities).

Blockchain Wallet Fees

It's worth noting that the Blockchain Wallet employs a system known as dynamic fees, which means that the cost charged for each transaction might vary depending on various factors. The magnitude of the charge is determined by the transaction size and the network conditions at the time of the transaction. Miners, which are high-powered computers, can only handle a certain amount of transactions every block. Because the transactions with the highest fees are the most profitable, miners normally execute them first.

Blockchain Wallet offers a priority fee, which might result in the transaction being executed within an hour. There's also a standard price, which is less expensive but will certainly take more than an hour to complete. Customers can also tailor their fees. The transaction may be delayed or refused if the consumer sets the charge too low.

Wallet Security

Users should be concerned about wallet security since a hacked account might lose control of their assets. To secure user cash from any potential attacker, including the firm itself, Blockchain Wallet features numerous levels of protection.

Passwords

Blockchain Wallet accounts require passwords for user security, like other digital services. However, the Blockchain firm does not keep user credentials and cannot reset them if they are forgotten. This safeguard keeps firm insiders from stealing cryptocurrency. If a user forgets or loses their password, only a mnemonic seed is used to retrieve the account.

Mnemonics Seeds

A mnemonic seed is a random combination of English words that acts as a password replacement. If a user loses their phone or device access, the seed is used to recover the wallet, including any Bitcoins. Users' mnemonic seeds, like passwords, are not stored by the Blockchain firm, and the wallets may be retrieved even if the organization goes out of business since these seeds follow an industry standard.

Security methods are used in addition to the safeguards mentioned above, and several extra security features can help protect user wallets from outside threats. The Blockchain wallet allows users to employ two-factor authentication or IP whitelists to prevent logins from unknown devices, reducing the risk of phishing. It's also possible to prevent potential hackers from hiding their IP addresses by blocking access through the Tor network.

Best Crypto Wallet in 2022

Coinbase Wallet

Coinbase is a popular option especially for buying and selling of Bitcoin, ethereum, and litecoin globally.

ZenGo

ZenGo is a universal cryptocurrency wallet. Buy, trade, and earn up to 8% APY on BTC, ETH, and other cryptocurrencies (over 70 of the top cryptocurrencies). Enjoy unbreakable security and unparalleled customer service, with genuine support specialists available to solve any problem 24 hours a day, seven days a week.

Exodus

Exodus is merely a software platform; there is no independent due diligence or substantive examination of any Blockchain asset, cryptocurrency, digital currency, or associated cash.

MetaMask

MetaMask is a Bitcoin wallet that also functions as a gateway to Blockchain-based applications.

Trezor Wallet

Trezor is the most reliable and secured option to storing your Bitcoins.

Trust Wallet

Trust is an Ethereum mobile wallet and DApp browser that is easy, fast, and safe.

BitGo

BitGo is the world's leading institutional digital asset financial services provider, providing clients with security, compliance, custody, and liquidity. In 2013, BitGo introduced the first multi-signature hot wallet for institutional investors.

StakedWallet.io

Stakedwallet.io is a website that helps you manage your asset. Users will be able to earn using Proof-Of-Stake with this brand-new cryptocurrency wallet. The website also supports cryptocurrency exchange and has a 5-level referral and incentive structure.

Cainpayment Wallet

CoinPayments is a global payment gateway that enables clients to trade Bitcoin instantly, Ethereum, and Litecoin, including over 2,000 other cryptocurrencies. CoinPayments has been an industry pioneer since 2013, assisting businesses in accepting cryptocurrency payments with safe, quick, safe, and simple-to-integrate solutions.

MyEtherWallet

MyEtherWallet is a client-side utility that allows you to interact with the open-source blockchain.

Coinomi

Coinomi is a multi-asset wallet that prioritizes security and offers native support and actual ownership of 1770 currencies and tokens in 168 paper currency representations and 25 languages.

Jaxx

Jaxx is a wallet for Bitcoin, Bitcoin Cash, Ethereum, Ethereum Classic, Litecoin, Dash, Zcash, and many other cryptocurrencies and Blockchain assets. Jaxx allows you to trade, spend, and receive money.

Using Your Blockchain Wallet
Wallet ID for login

You'll need your Wallet ID, password, and any two-factor authentication you've configured to log into your wallet. Your Wallet ID is a username made up of a string of random letters and digits. Go to the 'General' tab in your Settings menu to discover it. Your Wallet

ID, despite its resemblance to an address, cannot be used to transfer or receive payments.

Checking your accounts

Your balances will always be visible in your wallet and dashboard. Do you want to view your balance in your preferred currency? The fiat money counterpart will be displayed when you click on your cryptocurrency value.

Sending and receiving cash

You'll need the recipient's receiving address or QR code to send money from your wallet. You may share your address or a QR code with the sender to make a request. While your Bitcoin and Bitcoin cash addresses will vary with each request, your ether address will remain the same.

Getting the most out of your transaction feed

Your most recent transactions will appear on your home screen, and you can see a complete transaction feed by clicking on the appropriate asset in your wallet's menu.

Takeaways

- A blockchain wallet is a type of cryptocurrency wallet that lets users manage several cryptocurrencies, such as Bitcoin and Ethereum.

- Hot and cold wallets are the two types of Blockchain wallets based on private keys. Hot wallets are similar to the wallets we use for everyday transactions, and they are user-friendly. Cold wallets are similar to vaults in that they securely hold cryptocurrency.

- The transaction fees charged by Blockchain Wallet are dynamic, meaning they can vary depending on factors such as transaction size.

- A variety of security elements in Blockchain Wallet help prevent theft, even by corporate insiders.

CHAPTER 7

BITCOIN

Basics

Bitcoin is a network-based decentralized digital currency. Every Bitcoin transaction is recorded and stored in a public log, and individuals may remain anonymous on the network by using encrypted keys. There are no intermediaries involved in transactions; therefore, there is no need to go through a bank. Also, the decentralized Bitcoin system is not owned by any government, financial institution, or central authority. This implies that no account numbers, names, or other identifying information are required to link Bitcoins to their owners.

Bitcoins are "mined" using computers to solve complex math puzzles rather than being printed like paper money. Creating Bitcoin is not straightforward; it requires a lot of computational power, which consumes much electricity. Miners are encouraged to generate Bitcoins since they are currently compensated with 12.5 Bitcoins for solving a mathematical challenge that creates a new Bitcoin. At the moment, a new Bitcoin is generated every ten minutes.

Digital Wallets

As previously described, a wallet is nothing more than a collection of addresses and the keys that let you access the monies stored inside. A digital wallet functions similarly to a virtual bank account, allowing users to send and receive Bitcoins. It is also used to pay for products, such as a car, or save money for a car loan.

The majority of Bitcoin wallets vary from bank accounts in that the owner is solely responsible for the funds' security. Users may choose from a variety of wallets, each with a different level of protection. Wallets are available in several formats, including online, desktop, mobile, hardware, and paper variants. Users may choose between several security settings to see which one best suits their needs.

An online or mobile wallet keeps track of all Bitcoin transactions, administers the user's wallets, and can even make transactions directly on the Bitcoin network. Coinbase is an excellent example of an online and mobile wallet that people trust to keep their cash safe. In contrast, a desktop wallet is an application that can be downloaded and installed on a laptop, allowing users to store and control their currencies.

Bitcoin Technology

A Blockchain is shared and maintains a public record of all transactions shared and held by everyone in the Bitcoin network. Blockchain technology ensures that network transactions are irrefutable and prevent duplicate Bitcoins transactions. Alternative uses of Blockchain technology may be found in various other businesses and sectors, such as fractional property ownership in real estate and peer-to-peer energy trading in the energy sector. Blockchain technology has sparked a new wave of innovative ventures to change how the world works and functions.

Bitcoin Blockchain

Bitcoin (BTC) and Blockchain are combined in the Bitcoin Blockchain. When centralized entities failed the world, a person or a group of persons known as Satoshi Nakamoto established the Bitcoin protocol in 2008 to decentralize the control of money. The Bitcoin white paper established computational principles that determined the Blockchain, a new distributed database. And in January 2009, the network was launched. Bitcoin, the most well-known cryptocurrency, was the catalyst for the development of Blockchain technology. Like the US dollar, cryptocurrency is a digital medium of exchange that uses encryption methods to oversee the creation of monetary units and verify financial transactions.

However, the Bitcoin Blockchain is considerably more than just a cryptocurrency. Most cryptocurrencies, including Bitcoin, are based on this technology. The Bitcoin Blockchain is unusual in that it verifies the accuracy of all transactions. Nothing is left out of the network because every action in the Blockchain is recorded. An activity is time-stamped and protected after it is recorded and saved in one of the information blocks, and the complete record is accessible to anybody in the system.

The Bitcoin Blockchain is decentralized, meaning it is neither held nor managed by a single entity, and it's spread across a large number of networked computers. A hash is a code found in the Bitcoin Blockchain. Each block in the Blockchain has its hash. Because each block contains its hash and the preceding block's hash, hashing allows every network user to identify each block and direct them to progress up the chain.

With this in mind, the Blockchain's most important components are records, block, hash, and chain. The Blockchain has two sorts of forms: block records and transactional records. A block comprises the most recent Bitcoin transactions that haven't been recorded in any earlier blocks. Transaction records contain asset, price, and ownership information registered, authorized, and settled in seconds across all nodes. In the Blockchain network, a hash is a fixed-length string formed after transforming any length of input data, a block is akin to a page in a ledger or record book, and a chain is a network of blocks linked together.

How to Invest in Bitcoin

If you are ready to jump into cryptocurrency, investing in bitcoin will be a good place to start. In five simple steps, here's how to invest in Bitcoin:

Sign up with a Bitcoin exchange

First, you must determine where you wish to purchase Bitcoin. The vast majority of Bitcoin investors use cryptocurrency exchanges. Because Bitcoin is an example of open-source technology, there is no particular official "Bitcoin" organization; nonetheless, Bitcoin transactions are accepted by several exchanges. These exchanges serve as intermediaries in Bitcoin investing, much like a stock brokerage.

Create a Bitcoin wallet

When you purchase a coin, it is deposited in a "wallet," where all your cryptocurrencies are stored. As we introduced in an early chapter, wallets are available in hot wallets and cold wallets. Your Bitcoin exchange and perhaps a third-party provider manages a hot wallet. When you open an account with a few exchanges, you will be given a hot wallet. Hot wallets are useful because they allow you to access your currencies through the internet via a software program.

Register your wallet with a financial institution

After getting your wallet, you must link it to your bank account. You may use this approach to buy and sell coins. Your Bitcoin exchange account may also be linked to your bank account.

Purchase a Bitcoin

You are now prepared to purchase Bitcoin. Everything you require will be available for purchase on your Bitcoin exchange. The essential question is how much Bitcoin you should buy. The worth of some coins is up to hundreds of dollars, yet exchanges allow you to buy fractions of a single coin for as little as $25. Investing in Bitcoin is very risky; thus, before making any purchases, you should thoroughly examine your risk tolerance and evaluate your investment strategy. In the following part, we'll go over this in further depth.

Maintain a record of your Bitcoin holdings

After purchasing Bitcoin, you may perform the following:

Use your coins to make online purchases.

Hold your coins for an extended period hoping that their value will increase.

Use your coins for day trading—buying and selling coins with other Bitcoin owners, which may be done on a cryptocurrency exchange.

Your Bitcoin exchange will provide everything you need to purchase and sell coins.

How to Invest in Bitcoin

Bitcoin may be purchased in many ways, both directly and indirectly. You may start by investing in a firm that uses Bitcoin technology. Although Bitcoin is a risky investment, several businesses sell goods that use Bitcoin and Blockchain technology. The Amplify Transformational Data Sharing ETF is one of the numerous exchange-traded funds (ETFs) that incorporate shares from different Blockchain-related firms (BLOK). You're not investing in cryptocurrency directly but rather in the corporate stocks of firms that use Bitcoin. It's less risky, and most ETFs in this category outperform the market.

Second, you can participate in Bitcoin mining, allowing your computer to act as a node for the public ledger. Bitcoin miners are compensated with genuine Bitcoin in exchange for their contributions. You might be able to get free Bitcoin without ever purchasing it. Aside from what was previously said, let's look at some of the most common methods individuals are investing in Bitcoin today and what it means for investors.

Buying Bitcoin on its Own

Buying Bitcoin on its own is the most apparent Bitcoin investing method. Purchasing Bitcoin directly through an app such as Coinbase gives investors "physical" possession of the asset. Coinbase allows investors to buy Bitcoin and keep it in their encrypted wallets, which is a crucial distinction to make. Therefore, investors will have access to the asset's price performance and the ability to utilize it as a currency in later transactions. Holding Bitcoin on its own isn't that different from owning any other cryptocurrency, excluding the wildly fluctuating value.

It's worth noting that not every online platform or application allows investors to purchase Bitcoin on its own. People can invest in Bitcoin using online trading services like Robinhood, but they do not enable investors to possess Bitcoin (or its respective keys). Unlike Coinbase, Robinhood does not provide investors with "keys" to their Bitcoin holdings, allowing them to move the funds to their wallets. Therefore, investing in Bitcoin using Coinbase gives investors the ability to hold the asset and use it as a currency. On the other hand, Robinhood investors may only profit from price fluctuations in their accounts and cannot transfer their assets to an encrypted wallet. Before investing in any Cryptocurrency, investors should familiarize themselves with the limits of their trading platforms.

Greyscale's Bitcoin Investment Trust (GBTC)

Greyscale's Bitcoin Investment Trust, founded in 2013, has risen to the top of the Bitcoin sector. Greyscale focused on democratizing Bitcoin for the public to become a trusted name in a fast-developing market. While Bitcoin is already decentralized, Greyscale expands the number of individuals who can use the new digital money. Greyscale is a capital market investing platform that creates transparent, familiar investment instruments for a rising asset class with limitless upside.

Greyscale's present success is due to its efforts to make Bitcoin more accessible to the general public. Greyscale aided in bridging the gap between the educated and the misinformed. Greyscale accomplished this by making it easier than ever to invest in Bitcoin. Greyscale, for example, permits Bitcoin to be held in IRAs, Roth IRAs, and other brokerage and investor accounts.

Amplify the ETF for Transformational Data Sharing (BLOK)

The Amplify Transformational Data Sharing ETF is an exchange-traded fund that trades on the stock market, as its name indicates. On the secondary market, investors can buy BLOK shares to expand their exposure to Bitcoin. BLOK is an actively managed ETF that focuses on Blockchain technology. As a result, fund managers continuously look for Blockchain-related firms to invest in. As a result, everyone who buys BLOK is buying a basket of Blockchain technology businesses. While BLOK does not provide investors with direct access to Bitcoin, it does give them access to companies that leverage Blockchain and its transformative data-sharing technology.

Bitwise 10 Private Index Fund (BITW)

A Bitwise 10 Private Index Fund investment is a Bitwise 10 Large Cap Crypto Index investment. The Bitwise 10 Large Cap Crypto Index, for those unaware, measures the performance of the ten most significant Cryptocurrency assets on the market. As a result, investors who purchase shares in this fund will be investing in the top ten "crypto-assets," as determined by free-float market capitalization. Investors will see gains proportional to the number of shares they hold if the assets perform well.

Bitcoin Mining

Bitcoin mining is the process of producing valid blocks that add transaction data to Bitcoin's (BTC) public ledger, known as a Blockchain. It is an essential part of the Bitcoin network since it addresses the "double-spend problem." The double-spend problem relates to the necessity to agree on transaction history. Bitcoin ownership can be mathematically confirmed using public-key cryptography. However, cryptography cannot ensure that a coin hasn't already been given to someone else.

An agreed-upon ordering must be established to create a shared history of transactions based on when each transaction was completed, for example. Nevertheless, external input might be controlled by whoever supplies it, necessitating participants' faith in that third party. Mining (blockchain mining in particular) takes advantage of economic incentives to create a secure and accurate method of data organizing. Third parties who arrange transactions are decentralized and compensated for good conduct. However, any wrongdoing leads to a loss of economic resources, at least as long as most people are honest.

In Bitcoin mining, this result is produced by building a series of blocks that could be mathematically shown to have been stacked in the appropriate sequence with a certain level of resource commitment. The approach is based on the mathematical characteristics of a cryptographic hash, which would be a standardized form of data encoding. Because hashes are one-way encryption mechanisms, decrypting them to their input data is nearly impossible until every possible combination is evaluated until the result matches the stated hash.

Bitcoin miners work in this way: they cycle through billions of hashes per second until they locate one that meets a "difficulty" criterion. Because the difficulty and the hash are huge integers represented in bits, the condition states that the hash must be less than the difficulty. Every 2016 Bitcoin block — or about two weeks — the difficulty is re-adjusted to keep a consistent block time, which refers to how long it takes to locate each new block when mining.

Miners create a hash used to identify each block and is made from the data present in the block header. The Merkle root — another aggregated hash that incorporates the signatures of all transactions in that block — and the previous block's unique hash are the most crucial parts of the hash. This implies that changing even the slightest component of a block will affect its predicted hash and the hash of every subsequent block. This wrong Blockchain version would be immediately rejected by nodes, safeguarding the network from meddling.

The approach ensures that Bitcoin miners put in actual labor — the time and power spent hashing through all available combinations — by imposing a difficulty requirement. Bitcoin's consensus system is dubbed "proof-of-work." Malicious actors have no choice but to recreate the network's full mining power to attack it, which would cost billions of dollars in Bitcoin.

Bitcoin mining is akin to gold mining in many ways. Crypto mining (in the case of Bitcoin) is a computer function that generates new Bitcoin and keeps track of transactions and ownership. Bitcoin and gold mining both require a lot of energy and may yield a lot of money.

Takeaways

- Bitcoin is decentralized digital money that runs on a network.

- Users should instantly store Bitcoins in a "digital wallet" after purchasing them on an exchange.

- A wallet is nothing more than a collection of addresses and the keys that let you access the funds stored inside.

- The digital wallet functions similarly to a virtual bank account, allowing users to send and receive Bitcoins.

- Bitcoin may be purchased in various ways, both directly and indirectly. You may engage in Bitcoin mining or invest in a firm that uses Bitcoin technology.

- Bitcoin mining is the process of producing valid blocks that add transaction data to bitcoins's public ledger, known as a Blockchain.

CHAPTER 8

CRYPTOCURRENCY

Meaning

Cryptocurrency, often referred to as crypto-currency or crypto, refers to any digital or virtual currency that uses encryption to protect transactions. Cryptocurrencies lack a central issuing or governing entity and instead rely on a decentralized system to track transactions and generate new units. Cryptocurrency is a digital means of payment that does not rely on banks for transaction verification. It is a peer-to-peer system through which anyone can send and receive money anywhere. Cryptocurrency payments exist exclusively as digital entries to an online database identifying individual transactions instead of actual money carried about and exchanged in the real world. Transactions involving cryptocurrency are documented in a public ledger, and the cryptocurrency coin is stored in digital wallets.

Blockchain and Cryptocurrency Mechanism

The terms Blockchain and cryptocurrency are sometimes used interchangeably. Although they are two entirely different technologies, they are inextricably linked. Blockchain, a digitalized, decentralized public ledger, is a database of digital information, or blocks, held across a network of computers. When verified transactions occur, the data is saved in blocks, which are added to the chain when complete. The Blockchain is used to run cryptocurrency since it is a decentralized, digital system.

Blockchain is a fundamental aspect of cryptocurrencies rather than being an optional technology. Cryptocurrencies have fueled the growth and development of Blockchain, as crypto relies on its network to function. Blockchain, nevertheless, is not limited to cryptocurrency applications. The technology is not limited to the financial industry; it provides various solutions that have already disrupted and will continue to disrupt many businesses in the years ahead.

The names have become synonymous because the first Blockchain was the database on which every Bitcoin (the first cryptocurrency) transaction was kept. Blockchain was not identified as such when it was initially introduced in 2009. It got its name from how transactions were organized into data blocks and then linked together using a mathematical process that generates a hash code. The idea of a cryptographically safe chain of information blocks was conceived in 1982 and perfected in the early 1990s. Still, this groundbreaking initial coin propelled the system to popularity.

How to Buy Cryptocurrency

You might be wondering how can you buy cryptocurrency safely. Typically, there are three processes involved, and these are the following:

Step 1: Choose a platform

The first step is to select a platform on which to work. In general, you can use either a regular broker or a cryptocurrency trading platform:

Traditional Brokers

These online brokers enable you to buy and sell cryptocurrencies and other financial assets such as bonds, equities, and exchange-traded funds (ETFs). These platforms are recognized for their low trading fees but lack crypto functionality.

Exchanges

There are numerous cryptocurrency exchanges to choose from, each with its collection of cryptocurrencies, wallet storage options, interest-bearing account alternatives, and other features. Many exchanges charge Asset-based fees.

When comparing different platforms, consider which cryptocurrencies are offered, the fees they charge, their security features, storage and withdrawal options, and any educational resources.

Step 2: Depositing funds into your account

After deciding on a platform, you must fund your account before beginning trading. Although it differs by platform, most crypto exchanges allow users to purchase crypto with fiat (government-issued) currencies like the US dollar, British pound, or Euro using their debit or credit cards. Credit card transactions of cryptocurrency are considered risky, and some exchanges prohibit them. Some credit card companies also do not allow cryptocurrency transactions. This is because cryptocurrencies are highly volatile, and risking going into debt – or paying huge credit card transaction fees – for certain assets is not advised.

Some websites accept ACH and wire transfers as well. Payment methods accepted and the time required to deposit or withdraw money differ for each platform. Similarly, depending on the payment method, the time required for deposits varies. Fees are an important factor as well. Transaction costs for deposits and withdrawals, as well as trading fees, may be included. Fees will differ based on the payment method and platform used, so do your research ahead of time.

Step 3: Making a purchase

You can place an order through your broker or exchange's website or mobile interface. To purchase cryptocurrencies, go to "buy," select the order type, input the number of coins you want to purchase, and complete the order. Orders to "sell" are processed in the same way.

Step 4: Store your cryptocurrency

Once you have obtained cryptocurrency, you must store it safely to protect it from hackers or theft. Coins are frequently held in physical hardware, cryptocurrencies, or online software that securely stores your cryptocurrency's private keys. Some exchanges offer wallet services, letting you keep your funds on the platform. However, not all exchanges or brokers will provide you with a wallet right away. There are numerous wallet providers from which to choose.

Use Cases

Websites devoted to technology and e-commerce

Like newegg.com, AT&T, and Microsoft, several tech companies accept cryptocurrency on their platforms. Overstock was one of the first online retailers to accept Bitcoin, and it is also accepted by Rakuten, Shopify, and Home Depot.

Luxury goods

Some high-end retailers accept cryptocurrency as payment. Bitdials, for example, takes Bitcoin in exchange for Rolex, Patek Philippe, and other high-end clocks.

Cars

Some vehicle dealerships, ranging from mass-market to high-end luxury brands, now accept cryptocurrencies as payment.

Insurance

AXA, a Swiss insurer, announced in April 2021 that it has begun accepting Bitcoin as payment for all of its insurance lines, except life insurance (due to regulatory issues). Premier Shield Insurance, which provides house and automobile insurance plans in the United States, accepts Bitcoin for premium payments and cash.

Cryptocurrency Frauds

Unfortunately, cryptocurrency fraud is on the rise. Scams with cryptocurrency include the following:

Virtual Ponzi Schemes

Cryptocurrency fraudsters create the illusion of high returns by repaying old investors with money from new investors by offering phony chances to invest in cryptocurrencies. One fraudulent business, BitClub Network, had generated more than $700 million when its perpetrators were prosecuted in December 2019. Scammers pose as millionaires or well-known figures on the internet, promising to treble your virtual currency investment but instead stealing what you provide. They may even use messaging apps or chat forums to disseminate fake news that a well-known businessperson is a supporter of a specific cryptocurrency. After urging investors to buy and driving up the price, the fraudsters sell their holdings, and the currency loses value.

Virtual Currency Scams

The FBI has issued a warning about a new trend in online dating scams in which some artists convince people they meet on dating apps or social media to invest or trade in virtual currencies. The FBI's Internet Crime Complaint Centre received over 1,800 reports of crypto-focused romantic scams in the first seven months of 2021, with losses reaching $133 million. Likewise, criminals may pose as legitimate virtual currency traders or set up fraudulent exchanges to scam customers. Deceptive sales pitches for cryptocurrency-based individual retirement plans are another type of crypto fraud. Then there's basic cryptocurrency hacking, which involves hackers gaining access to people's digital wallets and stealing their virtual money.

Tips for Investing in Cryptocurrency

Every investment has some level of risk, and however, some experts say cryptocurrency is one of the riskier financial options available. If you're considering investing in cryptocurrencies, these tips will help you make an informed decision.

Research exchanges

Learn about cryptocurrency exchangers before you invest. There are over 500 exchanges to choose from, according to estimates. Do your research, read reviews, and consult with more experienced investors before deciding.

Learn how to keep your cryptocurrency secure

If you buy cryptocurrency, you must keep it safe. You could save it within a digital wallet or through an exchange. While there are numerous wallets, each contains its own set of benefits, technological requirements, and security measures. You should conduct proper research on storage choices before investing, just as you would on exchanges.

Diversify your investment portfolio

Diversification is critical to any successful investment strategy and is true for cryptocurrency. Don't put all of your money into Bitcoin because it's a well-known option. There are numerous options, and it is advisable to diversify your portfolio through investment in other currencies.

Prepare for volatility

The cryptocurrency market is highly volatile, so be prepared for ups and downs. Prices will change wildly. If your financial portfolio or mental health cannot handle it, cryptocurrency may not suit you. Cryptocurrency is currently popular and is considered very speculative. Be prepared for the challenges that come with making a new investment. If you decide to participate, do your research beforehand and begin with a bit of investment.

Best Cryptocurrency in 2022
Luckyblock

In a nutshell, this cryptocurrency project aims to overhaul the global lottery industry. The protocol does this by decentralizing the lottery process through Blockchain technology. The main idea is that everyone may partake in lottery games without passing through a centralized operator from their own home. All game actions are regulated and carried out through smart contracts to ensure that Luckyblock provides its participants with integrity and authenticity. This ensures that all lottery games are accurate and fair, with no possibility of tampering with the results by internal or external actors. If you are interested in investing in Luckyblock, you can acquire the project's digital token, which is presently in the pre-launch phase.

Shiba Inu

Shiba Inu debuted in August 2020, and its rapid rise in such a short time would be nothing short of amazing. This digital currency was valued at $0.000000000078 at the beginning of the year 2021, according to Coinmarketcap. The same cryptocurrency peaked at $0.0000312 in November 2021. This means Shiba Inu profited by almost 40 million percent in less than one year of trading.

Although gains of such magnitude are improbable, this token still has much upside potential. Shiba Inu is listed across all trading platforms, and the general market's interest in this crypto asset. Not only do Binance, Huobi, Crypto.com, and Coinbase fall within this category, but so does eToro. As a result, the daily trade volume on Shiba Inu sometimes exceeds $3 billion.

Terra

When considering the best new cryptocurrencies to buy in 2022, many projects that offer a hedge against unfavorable markets should be considered. After all, when Bitcoin falls, it tends to drag down the border markets. A handful of digital assets, like Terra and its underlying LUNA cryptocurrency, have a history of outperforming gloomy markets. For those new to this project, the Terra protocol is in charge of ensuring the stability of Terra stablecoins, linked to fiat currencies such as the US dollar and Japanese yen. Those who use the Terra platform can receive incentives for staking and have a say in the protocol's destiny via governance.

Yearn.finance

Early contributors to this decentralized enterprise received even bigger rewards in 2021. Those who invested in Yearn.finance at the beginning of 2021, for example, were paid approximately $22,000 per token. Only five months later, the same digital currency surpassed a price of $93,000. This corresponds to a profit increase of about 320 percent. It's worth mentioning that, despite the high price of Yearn.finance, tokens can be fragmented in the same manner that Bitcoin can.

It is a decentralized platform specializing in crypto-based financing for those unfamiliar with its services. Put another way; the platform brings borrowers and investors together to construct a completely decentralized financial system.

PancakeSwap

In 2022, PancakeSwap is a cryptocurrency to consider investing in. PancakeSwap is a decentralized exchange that started in late 2020. Users can buy and sell digital tokens on the exchange without using a third party. Furthermore, it is typically the primary point of contact for freshly issued cryptocurrencies dependent on the Binance Smart Chain. PancakeSwap's platform has attracted millions of traders, including billions of dollars in frozen liquidity.

We particularly applaud PancakeSwap's expansion into other Bitcoin staking and farming areas. CAKE, the cryptocurrency's native digital token, was valued at less than $1.10 in September 2020. CAKE peaked at around $44 in mid-2021 but has since dropped to $12 as the year comes to an end. This does, however, provide an excellent starting place for those interested in acquiring this digital currency going forward.

Takeaways

- Cryptocurrency is any digital or virtual currency that employs encryption to safeguard transactions.

- Cryptocurrencies function without a central issuing or regulating body; instead, they rely on a decentralized system to track transactions and create new units.

- Cryptocurrencies are dependent on the Blockchain, a distributed public database that keeps track of all transactions and is updated by currency holders.

- Once you've acquired bitcoin, you'll need to keep it safe from hackers and theft. Cryptocurrency is usually kept in crypto wallets.

- Learn about bitcoin exchanges before you invest. There are around 500 exchanges to select from. Before deciding, do your homework, study reviews, and speak with more experienced investors.

CHAPTER 9

NFTS

Meaning of NFT

An NFT is a fungible and interchangeable unit of digital data kept on the Blockchain (i.e., one is no different than another, like any one-dollar bill is not different from another one-dollar bill in value or meaning). NFTs are one-of-a-kind and non-replicable. NFTs use Blockchain technology to give verifiable proof of ownership of the object with which the NFT is linked. An NFT is essentially a digital certificate of authenticity. NFTs have been linked to easily reproducible goods like images, movies, music, and other sorts of digital assets, as well as more ephemeral commodities like a labeled moment in time, such as NBA Top Shot, which sells NFTs for amazing plays in NBA games, or Jack Dorsey, who sold an NFT for the first tweet. Purchase of an NFT does not obligate to confer any of the stated intellectual property rights (for example, copyright) in the subject matter of the NFT, just as acquiring a signed and limited edition copy of an image does not necessarily grant the purchaser copyright ownership of the image. A smart contract connected with the NFT may transfer the underlying intellectual property rights (or a portion of them). However, you must take proper care to ensure that the smart contract does not contradict the rules of the website or platform from which the NFT is made or acquired.

Role of Blockchain in NFT Development

NFTs may be issued or "minted" on various Blockchains. The most popular are Ethereum and Solana. Although Ether is a cryptocurrency, its Blockchain, Ethereum, also enables NFTs, which contain extra data about the digital file or other unique things to which they are linked. This distinguishes them from the ETH cryptocurrency, which merely stores the amount, transaction date, sender, and receiver on the Blockchain. The NFT, like Bitcoin, is controlled by a secret encryption key. The rights to the cryptocurrency or NFT are also lost or stolen if that key is lost or stolen. Many people like NFTs because they have the potential to generate additional revenue streams from an image, audio, or other digital files, as well as the opportunity for the NFT's creator to earn royalties on any subsequent sales of the NFT, which is usually not the case when selling unique items through other traditional methods. There are possible disadvantages to NFTs, such as that producing them (known as "minting") varies greatly, sometimes costing more than the NFT's value.

Furthermore, there may be ambiguity about what rights are connected with an NFT and doubts about the legitimacy of some NFTs. Notably, there have already been some high-profile legal disputes over whether an NFT minter has the requisite rights (such as licenses or personal rights) to generate the NFT in the first place. When minting, purchasing, or selling an NFT, employ prudence and diligence, just as you would with any other transaction.

Top Blockchains in NFT Development
Ethereum

Despite intense competition from other Blockchains, Ethereum has won the race for crypto and NFTs. It is the most extensively used Blockchain for minting NFTs, no doubt, because of how straightforward it is to operate. Another factor that added to its popularity is the large number of major NFT markets that use the Ethereum network, such as OpenSea, Rarible, and Decentraland, which all implement the ERC721 standard. When it comes to establishing non-fungible tokens, this Ethereum standard is one of the most reliable. However, it may not be the optimal network for those searching for lower gas prices. As demand for the Ethereum Blockchain grows, the cost of minting NFTs has risen, causing congestion and scalability issues in the past, not to mention the controversy it has faced over its proof-of-work system, which is a highly energy-intensive option for minting NFTs and settling network transactions.

Binance Smart Chain

As previously said, Ethereum has encountered several difficulties, prompting consumers to seek cheaper and even quicker alternatives. Binance Smart Chain is a Blockchain platform that runs alongside the Binance Chain network, specializing in smart-contract-based applications and supporting the Ethereum Virtual Machine (EVM) while retaining high transaction speeds and cheap gas fees. Because of its EVM compatibility, this Blockchain can handle a wide range of Ethereum DApps and tools, giving developers and consumers more options. The Binance Smart Chain is compatible with token standards such as the BEP2E token and the ERC-20 token (ETH), and the Binance Coin, the company's cryptocurrency (BNB).

Polygon

Polygon is a Blockchain that has earned a reputation for being one of the most dependable and cost-effective Blockchains available. Polygon NFTs are incorporated into the world's largest NFT marketplace, OpenSea, and some of the most popular NFT-based games, such as Aavegotchi and Polychain Monsters, leverage Polygon's scaling technology to ensure more dynamic experiences. The 'lazy minting' option, which means there are no upfront charges when producing NFTs, is a feature that people like. When an NFT is sold, a cost must be paid. Polygon is built for efficiency like many other Blockchain networks, with near-zero transaction costs, rapid settlement times, and a low-energy solution.

Solana

Despite being a new Blockchain, Solana has experienced a huge increase in acceptance, putting it in direct rivalry with Ethereum and Cardano. It's easy to see why crypto and digital art enthusiasts have begun minting NFTs on this chain. Solana has a great reputation for being a high-efficiency Blockchain that can handle 65,000 TPS while keeping fees around $0.01. Solana is the first Blockchain to integrate proof-of-history (PoH) and proof-of-stake (PoS) consensus processes, allowing for faster-than-average transaction and smart contract validation speeds. Another appealing feature is scalability, as seen by the rapid expansion of the Solana ecosystem, which currently includes, among other things, some of the major NFT platforms such as Solanart and Magic Eden. Furthermore, our Blockchain emits less carbon (the developer claims one Solana transaction consumes less energy than two Google searches). You may also be familiar with Solana due to its native cryptocurrency, SOL, whose value has risen lately.

Flow

Flow focuses on supporting game and Metaverse NFTs and assets such as digital collectibles, drawing on the extensive expertise of its creator, Dapper Labs, which has had remarkable success with projects such as CryptoKittes, Dapper Wallet, and, of course, the NBA Top Shot. Flow is a high-performance Blockchain with various integration and interoperability capabilities that make it particularly appealing to decentralized applications (Dapps), such as NFT markets. Furthermore, anybody may become a validator (also known as a miner) for the Flow Blockchain without additional criteria, such as specialized equipment, making joining Flow a simple process. Furthermore, the proof-of-stake method is used on this Blockchain, which keeps costs down while assuring that the network is environmentally sustainable. Other distinguishing features include:

- Transaction completion
- Upgradeable smart contract features
- Human-readable security
- Smart account recovery options

Cardano

Cardano is a distributed proof-of-stake Blockchain created by Charles Hoskinson, co-founder of Ethereum. The platform focuses on scalability and efficiency while allowing for powerful applications and transaction settlement in ADA, the platform's native token. Cardano was also created to become an environmentally sustainable Blockchain. Its ability to secure high performance at 65,000 transactions per second is one of its primary features, making it one of the quickest Blockchains accessible. As if that wasn't amazing enough, Hydra, the company's future Layer 2 scaling technology, could push that figure up to 2 million TPS. Compared to the competition, the transaction fees on this Blockchain are likewise relatively cheap. It has Ethereum Virtual Machine compatibility, just like the Binance Blockchain, to enable Ethereum-based smart contracts and DApps.

How to Buy and Sell NFTs

Non-fungible tokens may be purchased on several NFT exchanges, including Rarible, OpenSea, and ultrarare.

Here's how you can buy some using Rarible:

Step 1

Visit Rarible.com and select the 'Connect' option in the upper right corner, then Log in using the wallet you want to connect to the platform from here. Before you can log in, you must first agree to the terms of service. In this example, let's assume we're using Metamask, a popular web and mobile wallet.

Step 2

Once you've logged in, check through the platform for the NFT you want to buy. Regardless of the NFTs, the procedure remains the same (assuming it is available to purchase). Click the 'Buy now' button after choosing the NFT you want to buy.

Step 3

A confirmation box will appear, requesting that you double-check the order's information. Click the 'Proceed to the payment button to go to the last step.

Step 4

Your wallet will send you a notification asking you to authenticate the transaction. If you want to continue, simply confirm the transaction, and it will be completed. Your NFT will be transferred to your Ethereum address immediately and will be yours to keep once validated.

Choosing the Best Blockchain for your NFTs

When looking for the ideal Blockchain for NFT, there are a lot of factors to consider. The following are examples of this:

Possibility of forking

NFTs are extremely expensive due to their rarity and distinctiveness. Hard forks potentially jeopardize these features, as the purity of NFTs is called into question if they are copied. The ownership of the assets is at stake. Furthermore, NFTs on the 'old' chain may have their value completely decimated. As a result, NFTs and NFT markets must be built on fork-resistant Blockchains.

Smart, robust contracts

When it comes to the total security provided by Blockchain technology, the resilience of its smart contracts is a crucial element. For this reason, writing bug-free, clean, and secure code is essential. Smart contracts must go through extensive testing to ensure that you get the most out of them. NFT marketplace consumers and developers can only be certain that downtime, hacks, and breaches are at a minimum.

Token development and transaction fees

In addition to the issues we've just mentioned, cost-effectiveness is something else. When performing NFT-based transactions, you'll need cost-effective solutions because they won't necessarily require trading in million-dollar art items. Micro-transactions account for a significant portion of NFT-based transactions, and they can include card games, digital collectibles, and in-game digital assets.

Naturally, no one will be ready to pay exorbitant fees for such transactions. As a result, you'll need to keep the cost as low as possible to ensure uptake and usage. As a result, there is a demand for reduced Blockchain development costs, particularly in the case of NFT markets. As a result, the Blockchain's fee structure for NFTs must be carefully studied, and some don't require any payment.

Security

Of course, we can't discuss the many variables to consider while looking for a Blockchain for NFT development without considering the crucial aspect of security. Man-in-the-middle attacks and 51 percent attacks are two types of attacks that may be used to compromise Blockchains. Platforms using proof of work consensus techniques are far more vulnerable to attacks in which hackers seize control of a large proportion of the network's computing power.

Loss of access, data, and money are unavoidable consequences of such an attack, ultimately jeopardising decentralisation. As a result, it's critical to look for a Blockchain with alternative consensus processes, like proof of stake, that don't need mining.

Speed of transactions

Last but not least, you must evaluate the transaction's speed. When it comes to the success of a digital system, speed is one of the most critical factors, especially when it comes to value transfer and domains, including storage. However, speed should not be exchanged for low levels of security or significant fees, as is the case with many Blockchains, so keep that in mind.

Because Blockchains are immutable by design, faster execution implies attackers will have a shorter window of opportunity. If you can find a Blockchain that can do this while maintaining decentralization, you have undoubtedly discovered the ideal environment for NFT development.

BAYC New Apecoin

Yuga Labs has had a particularly explosive year, even among the fastest-growing crypto businesses. Yuga Labs is announcing a new alliance for a play-to-earn gaming title centered on the much-hyped ApeCoin token and supposedly seeking funding at $5 billion. Some very precise legal maneuverings will be required to preserve regulatory compliance while building this economy. The SEC has steered away from NFT projects for the most part — but not entirely — but crypto businesses selling tokens that function as unregistered securities have been a focus of their attention.

As a result, Yuga Labs is taking steps to distance itself from the token's launch, which will be handled by an organization called ApeCoin DAO, which comprises council members involved in the NFT project and are not Yuga Labs employees or executives. The APE Foundation will supervise ApeCoin DAO decisions and control the ApeCoin DAO. The DAO will also have official BAYC branding, which Yuga Labs will "give" to it in the style of a 1/1 NFT of a blue Bored Apes logo. The ApeCoin DAO's council members are Reddit co-founder Alexis Ohanian, Sound Ventures' Maaria Bajwa, FTX's Amy Wu, Animoca's Yat Siu, and Horizen Labs' Dean Steinbeck.

Holders of DAO tokens will be able to vote on DAO decisions, while the special counsel will carry out the community's choices. Even though Yuga will not publicly launch the Ethereum-based token, the founders of the firm and BAYC project will own around a quarter of the total token supply and owners of Bored Apes and Mutant Apes NFTs, will receive a cumulative 15% of the total token allocation.

The following is a breakdown of the 1 billion APE coin token distribution:

- Bored Apes Yacht Club's founders will earn 8% of the proceeds.
- The Yuga Labs team will receive 16% of the funding (a portion equal to 1 percent of the entire token supply donated to the Jane Goodall Foundation Legacy Foundation).

- 14% of the tokens will be distributed to "launch contributors," who are most likely Yuga partners and investors.

- Owners of the Bored Apes collections and Mutant Apes collections will get 15% of the asset.

- 47% will be distributed over time as part of the DAO's "ecological fund."

The full breadth of ApeCoin's functionality is presently unknown. Still, it will be used as in-game cash for several of Yuga Labs' upcoming games, including a previously unreleased project created with San Francisco-based gaming studio nWay. The firm has already released various fight games based on IP like Power Rangers and the WWE. Yuga's entry into gaming is an essential aspect of the BAYC brand's expansion plans, but Blockchain gaming is still a minor sector that the company hopes to develop.

BAYC NFT Platform Development

The Bored Ape Yacht Club (BAYC) is a non-fungible token (NFT) collection based on the Ethereum network. An algorithm procedurally creates profile photos of cartoon apes in this collection. Bored Ape Yacht Club's parent firm is Yuga Labs. The project kicked up with a live pre-sale on April 23, 2021. An exclusive online club, special in-person events, and intellectual property rights for the picture are available to owners of a Bored Ape NFT.

The NFT collection was developed by four guys who "went out to create some dope apes, test (their) talents and try to build something (crazy). Bored Ape NFTs, like other NFTs, made and used for digital art, seek to deliver "original" artwork to its owners. Owners of Bored Ape NFTs are said to have a unique unit of data stored on a digital Blockchain, which maintains its origins or sales history eternally. The collection consists of 10,000 distinct NFTs stored on the Ethereum Blockchain.

Bored Ape Yacht Club, an NFT platform similar to Bored Ape Yacht Club, is a novel approach to creating a trading environment that focuses mostly on building communities and expanding them with other users. Bored Ape Yacht Club will be comparable to the NFT platform, with numerous sets of NFT collectibles and use cases for these collectibles to build a chain trade. Users who meet the requirements for this membership get exclusive access to the restroom, and members will receive perks and access to special material as part of the membership program.

How Bored Ape Yacht NFT platforms Work

Themed platforms, such as Bored Ape Yacht Club and other NFT platforms, are available. The NFT markets also have a fantastic welcoming attitude for themed tokens or assets. To make themed NFTs, follow these procedures.

Step 1

Use Apes in the library to make NFTs. A limited amount of avatars and images of uninteresting ape-like items are available. These components should be themed differently.

Step 2

The trait library enables the bulk expansion engine to manufacture Bored Ape-like NFTs in vast quantities. Coolers, dresses, and other garments are added to the NFTs.

Step 3

After the NFT-like Bored Apes have been created, the removal engine may be used to trim them. All NFTs that are comparable will be removed as a result of this. Finally, you can mass-produce the whole collection of NFTs using NFT themes.

Step 4

Launch and sell the one-of-a-kind, theme-based NFTs. Many other features, such as a membership program that helps develop a community within the banking sector, might be added to the platform.

Advantages of Bored Ape NFT Platform

These NFTs are very popular, and many individuals in the crypto community have indicated an interest in investing in them.

Exploration with No Limits

The Bored Ape Yacht Club is an open-ended NFT platform. They may conduct transactions without using intermediaries or centralized nodes from anywhere on the planet.

The Most Effective Blockchain Integration

NFT platforms will be integrated into the main Blockchain platforms inside the crypto industry based on customer requirements.

Compatibility Across Chains

Because of the support of another major crypto-Blockchain, the NFT platform theme is well-equipped. As a result, Dapps from several Blockchains will be able to be integrated into the platform.

Multi-Platform Support

To increase the user market, Bored Ape Yacht Club NFT platform will be improved to be used on all devices and operating systems.

Takeaways

- An NFT is a fungible and interchangeable unit of digital data kept on the Blockchain instead of cryptocurrency, and they are one-of-a-kind and non-replaceable.

- NFTs use Blockchain technology to give verifiable proof of ownership of the object with which the NFT is linked.

- NFTs may be issued or "minted" on various Blockchains, the most popular Ethereum and Solana.

- There is a slew of NFT markets to choose from. The largest is OpenSea, which utilizes Ethereum as its primary currency and accepts more than 150 other payment tokens.

- The Bored Ape Yacht Club (also known as Bored Ape) is a non-fungible token collection based on the Ethereum network.

- Yuga Labs is announcing a new collaboration for a play-to-earn gaming product based on the much-hyped ApeCoin currency.

CHAPTER 10

METAVERSE

Meaning of Metaverse

Metaverse is a combination of the words "meta," which means "beyond," and "verse," which means universe. As a result, "Metaverse" refers to a virtual environment outside of reality. Because the Metaverse is a subset of the internet's progression, it cannot be considered static. For example, we've all gone through several stages of internet technology, from sending text-based communications to sharing memories through photographs, and finally, video-based online interactions. We've arrived in the Metaverse, which will give us a new and improved version of the internet, complete with a 3D virtual and augmented reality. It creates a virtual environment that mirrors the actual world and allows users to accomplish anything they can in it.

Employees may work in a virtual office, and students can enroll in online programs, individuals can shop, and many more fun activities. Metaverse is expected to improve today's Internet and its utility across numerous industries with these features.

Components of the Metaverse

Decentralized Blockchain-based Metaverse projects are the norm nowadays. Gaming platforms, NFT markets, and virtual product development platforms like Minecraft are examples of these projects.

Furthermore, some innovative Metaverse projects merge all of these platforms into a single project. However, the following are the essential elements of the Metaverse:

- To host the Metaverse, a high-bandwidth network of computers is necessary, as it functions independently of any centralized authority, allowing decentralized data transfer for reliable and real-time communications.

- Images, videos, text, music, 3D things, and 3D sceneries all have open and interoperable standards.

- HTML, JavaScript, WebXR, WebAssembly, WebGPU Shader language, and others are examples of open programming language standards required.

- Virtual reality headsets, smart glasses, Omni treadmills, industrial cameras, scanning sensors, and other virtual, augmented and mixed reality technologies are necessary to transport people to the Metaverse's virtual realm.

- Blockchain technology and smart contracts make transparent, censorship-resistant advantages and permissionless transactions possible.

- Computing power is used to execute data processing, artificial intelligence, and projection with speed and precision.

- 3D immersive simulations will support virtual space habitats that mimic real-world ecosystems.

- Payment gateways that accept digital payments in both crypto and fiat currency.

Role of Blockchain in the Metaverse

In today's context, the phrase "Metaverse" refers to a virtual place constructed using 3D technology within the new internet. This notion is intimately tied to recent technological advancements like Blockchain, augmented and mixed reality, NFT, etc. The user is immersed in a virtual realm where they can do anything in real life, such as visiting intriguing destinations, meeting people, acquiring art, and selling real estate. Experts agree that establishing a Blockchain-based Metaverse can create a fantastic virtual environment that will revolutionize how everyone involved interacts.

So, what exactly does Blockchain have to do with the Metaverse? Many Blockchain-based systems now employ non-fungible tokens and cryptocurrencies to create, own, and monetize decentralized digital assets, establishing an ecosystem for producing, holding, and monetizing digital assets. Due to the inherent flaws of centralized data storage, the Metaverse idea is inadequate without blockchain. The ability of blockchain to operate internationally as a digital source based on the concept of decentralization separates the Metaverse from the capabilities of the traditional internet, which takes the form of websites and apps. Without the intervention of a centralized entity, the blockchain-based Metaverse allows access to any digital place.

Blockchain Use Cases in the Metaverse

Blockchain may be used in various ways to build and operate the Metaverse. The following are some of the most common applications of this technology.

Gaming

Many Blockchain specialists believe that gaming will soon be where the Metaverse concept takes off. They believe that players' virtual assets will be offered in the form of non-fungible Metaverse tokens. In time, gaming will allow players to earn a real money that can be utilized as payment inside a certain ecosystem. For players, incorporating Blockchain technology into games implies that their assets will remain safe even if they exit the game, delete it, or suffer an unpleasant life event.

Much money is being put into this, and sophisticated technology developers are working hard to fill this gap. The game "The Sandbox," a virtual environment with an integrated Ethereum-based cryptocurrency, is the greatest illustration of a breakthrough development. Some popular companies in the real world are already present in the Sandbox Metaverse environment. "Axie Infinity," which boasts over a million active players, is one of the most popular contemporary Metaverse NFT games. This game has a unique feature in that players are rewarded with an internal currency that encourages new players to join.

According to many influential personalities, the Metaverse will be actively used by investors, developers, and ordinary users in the future years, including Mark Zuckerberg, the founder of Meta. We can fairly assume that the popularity of this notion will skyrocket soon.

Cryptocurrencies

Payment settlements are one of the most prominent applications of Blockchain technology in the Metaverse. Customers will soon be able to shop in virtual storefronts. We can be confident that Bitcoin will soon find its place in a decentralized environment. Consumption is continually expanding, and offline commerce progressively gives way to online businesses.

MANA, which is used to acquire virtual property in the game "Decentraland," is one of the Metaverse examples of the usage of virtual currency in the Metaverse. Million-dollar transactions are already taking place in this Metaverse, and it's only the beginning. Users will be able to purchase virtual equivalents of everything that can be bought in the actual world in the future. This technology will not be restricted to games: the rapidly growing DeFi niche might easily become a testbed for virtual lending, borrowing, investing, and trading in the Metaverse. As a result, the potential of cryptocurrency looks to be limitless.

NFTs

Non-fungible tokens, according to many analysts, will play an important role in the Metaverse. These coins will be utilized in digital art exchange, where they are currently widely used as proof of ownership of digital assets. Furthermore, NFTs have a huge potential for integration into any Metaverse crypto projects, including purchasing game assets, avatars, and other items. Furthermore, if this field develops further, non-fungible tokens will soon be used as proof of real estate ownership.

An NFT is, in a general sense, a key to certain sections of the Metaverse. Aside from that, tokens will ultimately be used as a prize in Metaverse NFT games (instead of fungible tokens). Non-fungible tokens will be used to give value to specific digital assets: this is critical since practically any digital asset may be copied indefinitely, and only a certificate of ownership embedded in a digital object can prove the legal owner's right.

Authentication of Self-identity

Self-identity authentication is done in the Metaverse in the same way as a social security number is assigned. The Blockchain stores all information about an individual user, including age, activity, attractiveness, and other attributes. This provides maximum openness and protects the Metaverse from illicit activity. Furthermore, self-identity authentication prevents the potential of someone in the virtual environment from committing criminal acts under a fake name.

Real Estate

Real estate is a significant digital asset in the Metaverse. The main issues here are how to value a virtual real estate asset and govern this market if the Metaverse is truly an unlimited digital realm. This is where the Metaverse Blockchain may be used as a register for all acts involving virtual real estate assets, such as creation, modification, acquisition, sale, or disposal.

To summarize, it is evident that, while the Metaverse and Blockchain have evolved as separate concepts when combined, their full potential is realized. The notions have complimentary purposes that will eventually have a synergetic effect: people will notice something fundamentally different, which will help to shift people's perceptions of virtual reality and the crypto Metaverse.

Top Blockchain and Crypto Projects in the Metaverse

Many developers are now implementing the Metaverse idea to real-world Blockchain applications. The top 5 Blockchain ecosystems are shown below.

The Sandbox

This NFT game is quite popular right now. It started as a simple mobile app, but it has grown into a sophisticated Ethereum-based Metaverse with its SAND coin. Users establish an avatar linked to an e-wallet that allows them to manage non-fungible tokens, an internal currency (SAND), and various other assets. The game includes an integrated "play-and-earn" mechanism that aims to boost the local economy even more.

Decentraland

Users may create avatars, buy and equip land plots, plan events, and produce digital content in this 3D Metaverse. Decentraland's internal economy is based on the Blockchain, which allows for digital identification and validation of in-game asset ownership, and virtual real estate is the game's major digital asset (LAND). Furthermore, the Metaverse contains a native ERC-20 cryptocurrency token (MANA) used as internal mutual settlement between the players.

Star Atlas

One of the most recent releases is the Metaverse "Star Atlas," based on multiplayer gaming goods that use DeFi and Metaverse Blockchain technology. "Star Atlas" allows gamers to buy digital assets like land, spacecraft, equipment, and crew. The POLIS monetary system has also been developed, which serves as the foundation for the in-game economy. Experts feel Star Atlas has a lot of promise because of the various innovations employed in its creation.

Enjin

Enjin is a one-of-a-kind Metaverse project. It runs on the Blockchain, but it also allows for the development of software and SDK for the quick construction of NFTs. A secure Ethereum-based NFT development platform is involved. By transforming Enjin NFT into ENJ Metaverse tokens, the method assures that digital assets are very liquid. Furthermore, because ENJ tokens are rare, their value and digital collectability are preserved.

Bloktopia

Bloktopia is a virtual reality Metaverse built on top of the Polygon Blockchain in which you may study, make money, play games, and create. Bloktopia has an integrated play-to-earn game powered by the internal Metaverse token BLOK and Adblok advertising options. You may also use Reblok to sell real estate, design your immersive gaming surroundings, and play various games in the Metaverse.

Takeaways

- The Metaverse is an Internet-based future evolution built on persistent, shared virtual environments in which people interact as 3D avatars.
- Blockchain technology may serve as the Metaverse's backbone, with interoperable NFT assets that may be used in many Metaverse locations.

- Many Blockchain-based systems now employ non-fungible tokens and cryptocurrencies to create, own, and monetize decentralized digital assets, establishing an ecosystem for producing, holding, and monetizing digital assets. Due to the inherent flaws of centralized data storage, the Metaverse idea is inadequate without blockchain.

- The ability of blockchain to operate internationally as a digital source based on the concept of decentralization separates the Metaverse from the capabilities of the traditional internet, which takes the form of websites and apps.

- Hardware and software are the two essential components of any Metaverse. All forms of controllers are included in the hardware component, allowing users to engage easily with virtual or augmented reality. We're talking about a digital environment with material available to the user in the case of software.

- Metaverse is a fantastic concept and the next significant step forward in digital socialization. Based on major IT companies' broad acceptance of the Metaverse, we should expect a bigger expansion in the following years.

CHAPTER 11

WEB 3.0

Basics of Web 3.0

Imagine a different kind of internet that correctly translates what you write and understands what you say, whether through text, speech, or other channel, and where all of the material you consume is more personalized than ever before. Web 3.0 is the recent version of the internet, and with the emergence of Blockchain networks and cryptocurrencies, it is steadily becoming a big adoption trend. This new version of the web takes a different approach from its predecessor, web 2.0, which serves as the backbone for platforms like Facebook and Twitter and e-commerce ecosystems like Amazon.

While web 2.0 has played an important role in the evolution of the internet, it has also raised serious concerns about user security and data privacy in recent years. Web 3.0 aims to overcome these concerns by establishing a decentralized internet where users may participate in ecosystem governance and profit from their data when it is monetized. In web 2.0, centralized parties have complete control over their consumers' data and income sharing. Currently, the crypto business is home to most of web 3.0's sophisticated advancements. This is because cryptocurrencies are designed on Blockchain networks with a decentralized design. Web 3.0 decentralized protocols, in theory, offer a peer-to-peer ecosystem, obviating the need for an intermediary. In addition, depending on the underlying algorithm, they are run and regulated by a community (miners or validators).

Features of Web 3.0

We need to look at the four essential features of web 3.0 to comprehend the next stage of the internet truly:

- 3D Graphics
- Ubiquity
- Semantic Web
- Artificial Intelligence

3D Graphics and Spatial Web

Web 3.0 is famous as the spatial web by some futurists because it intends to blur the real and digital borders by reinventing graphics technology and bringing three-dimensional virtual worlds into sharp relief. 3D graphics, unlike their 2D predecessors, provide a new degree of immersion not just in futuristic gaming applications like Decentraland but also in other industries such as real estate, health, e-commerce, and many others.

Ubiquity

Ubiquity is the ability to be everywhere simultaneously. For example, a person on Facebook can snap and post an image right away, making web 2.0 widely accessible because it can be seen by anyone, no matter where they are, as long as they can use the social media platform. Taking a step further, web 3.0 makes the internet available to anyone at anytime and anywhere so that they can use it to do things. No longer will internet-connected gadgets be confined to PCs and smartphones like web 2.0. IoT (Internet of Things) technology will bring out a lot of new types of smart devices, so they won't just be connected to the internet.

Semantic Web

The study of the link between words is known as semantic(s). According to Berners-Lee, the Semantic Web allows computers to evaluate large amounts of data from the web, such as content, transactions, and relationships between people. What would this look like in practice? Take these two statements as an example:

I love Bitcoin

1 <3 Bitcoin

Their syntax may change, but their semantics are essentially the same because semantics solely deals with the content's meaning or emotion. By analyzing data and applying semantics to the web, robots will be able to understand meaning and emotions. As a result of the improved data connectivity, internet users will enjoy a better experience.

Artificial Intelligence

According to Wikipedia, artificial intelligence (AI) is intelligence displayed by machines. Web 3.0 machines are clever because they can read and comprehend the meaning and emotions expressed by a set of data. Despite web 2.0 having similar abilities, it is still mostly made up of humans, making it easy for people to do things like biased product reviews, manipulating ratings, etc. For instance, online review sites such as Trustpilot enable users to offer a review on any product or service. Unfortunately, a business may easily hire many individuals to write excellent evaluations for its meritorious items. As a result, for the internet to give reliable data, it requires AI to learn how to distinguish the authentic from the fraudulent.

Relationship Between Blockchain and Web 3.0

The Bitcoin Blockchain and other protocols assisted in the development of networks in which hackers would have to break into several houses across the world to gain access to data in a single home. Blockchain lays the framework for web 3.0 by allowing data storage in multiple copies of the peer-2-peer network, the protocol assists in the formal definition of management rules. Furthermore, the protocol guides data security by demanding consensus from all network members. In exchange for their contributions to the network's security and upkeep, participants are rewarded with native network tokens.

When you analyze how Blockchain affects data structures in the backend of the web, it's evident that it's the foundation for web 3.0. Most crucially, it contributed to developing a governance layer that operates on top of the current internet. The governance layer can let two untrustworthy individuals create an agreement and settle transactions via the internet. Surprisingly, the possibilities of Blockchain in web 3.0 would mainly focus on enabling a backend revolution. Web 3.0 may be regarded as a series of Blockchain-based protocols intended to change the internet's backbone technologically. Most significantly, Blockchain may be thought of as a distributed world computer that will transform how we see the internet.

Evolution of Web 3.0 Technologies

The internet has changed significantly over time, and its current applications are nearly unrecognizable from its early days. The internet has progressed through three stages: Web 1.0, Web 2.0, and Web 3.0.

Web 1.0

The earliest version of the internet was known as web 1.0. Think of the read-only or syntactic web as web 1.0. Most participants are content consumers; however, the creators are generally web developers who create mostly text or graphic content websites. Web 1.0 was a phase that existed between 1991 and 2004. Websites provided static content rather than dynamic hypertext markup language in web 1.0. (HTML). The websites had little interactivity, and data and content were retrieved through a static file system rather than a database.

Web 2.0

The bulk of us has only seen the web in its current version, commonly referred to as web 2.0, or the interactive read-write and social web. To participate in the development process in the web 2.0 ecosystem, being a developer isn't required. Many programs are designed so that anyone can create them. You have the power to think and communicate your thoughts to the rest of the world. You may also upload a video to web 2.0 for millions of people to watch, engage with, and comment on; YouTube, Instagram, Facebook, Twitter, Flickr, and other social media platforms are examples of web 2.0 apps.

Companies may leverage web technologies such as HTML5, CSS3, and JavaScript frameworks such as ReactJs, AngularJs, VueJs, and others to create new concepts that enable users to contribute more to the social web. As a result, because web 2.0 is built around people, developers need to make way for them to be empowered and engaged.

Consider how different major apps such as Instagram, Twitter, LinkedIn, and YouTube were when they first began compared to how they are now. The following is a common approach used by all of these companies:

- The company releases an app.

- It enlists as many people as possible.

- The company's user base then generates the money.

Web 3.0

Web 3.0, commonly referred to as Semantic Web or read-write-execute, is the future of the web (started in 2010). Artificial Intelligence (AI) and Machine Learning (ML) enable computers to analyze data the same way humans do, allowing the intelligent production and dissemination of relevant information customized to individual users' needs. Although both encourage decentralization, there are some key distinctions between web 2.0 and web 3.0. Web 3.0 developers seldom develop and deploy apps that store data in a single database or run on a single server (usually hosted on and managed by a single cloud provider).

Web 3.0 applications are built on Blockchain, decentralized networks containing a hybrid of the two or numerous peer-to-peer nodes (servers). The term for these applications is decentralized apps (DApps), and you'll hear it a lot in the web 3.0 community. Participants in the network (developers) are rewarded for offering high-quality services, resulting in a robust and secure decentralized network.

Web 2.0 vs. Web 3.0

In the following ways, web 3.0 differs from and improves upon web 2.0 technology:

- Web 3.0 is a semantic and geographical platform, whereas web 2.0 is a social platform. Social connections and connectivity were the two most significant features that constituted web 2.0. Web 3.0, however, emphasizes the linkages between online assets to organically surface helpful content and resources (often powered by AI and ML).

- An oligopoly governs web 2.0, whereas web 3.0 is decentralized.

- Web 2.0 has been dominated by several technical behemoths that, unwittingly, operate as an oligopoly. Despite the advent of new industries and challenges, companies like FAANG (now MAANG since Facebook was renamed Meta) and Big Tech continue to dominate debates. However, web 3.0 is designed on the Blockchain, allowing for the necessary decentralization. This is aided by a well-balanced economy in which producers and consumers are compensated for their time, effort, and expertise.

- Web 2.0 caters to groups, but web 3.0 caters to individuals. Although this issue is minor, it has a significant impact. Web 2.0 strives to harness collective power due to its social nature, i.e., user groups and communities. This might lead to impersonal meetings and the propagation of fake news driven by collective emotion. However, web 3.0 focuses on identifying individual users, learning their preferences, and customized experiences to their preferences while maintaining transparency through Blockchain and open-source design.

- Web 2.0 is two-dimensional, but web 3.0 combines two- and three-dimensional worlds. Web 2.0 is two-dimensional, and web 2.0 resources are shown as two-dimensional objects even in virtual reality. Web 3.0, on the other hand, combines 2D and 3D to give a better user experience by employing immersive realities. Web 3.0 may be accessed from a far more comprehensive range of devices than only phones and PCs, enabling the production of 3D visuals that are truly immersive.

- Web 2.0 is the textual phase, while web 3.0 is the executable phase (The legible phase was web 1.0.). Web 1.0, the first generation, was all about acquiring information. Users could only see content on a static web page without interactivity or searchability. In the second generation, which brought significant interactive possibilities, users could now add to the corpus of online knowledge without having any technical expertise. They may also perform more complex tasks, including searching, selecting results, and inputting data. Web 3.0 is expected to be the internet's operational phase, with AI and machine learning enabling machine-to-machine interactions to find resources that fits user desires.

Web 3.0 Applications

A web 3.0 ability to ingest a massive amount of data and translate it into factual information and practical activities for users is a common requirement for the new phase of the internet. These apps are still in the early stages of development, which means a lot of room exists for improvement and is far from how web 3.0 apps may operate. Amazon, Apple, and Google are just a few companies developing or converting existing products into web 3.0 apps. Web 3.0 features are used by Siri and Wolfram Alpha, two apps.

Siri

Apple's voice-controlled AI assistant has grown in sophistication and capabilities since its debut in the iPhone 4S model. Siri uses speech recognition and artificial intelligence to execute complex and personalized commands. Siri and other AI assistants such as Amazon's Alexa and Samsung's Bixby can now understand and reply to requests such as "where is the nearest burger store" or "schedule an appointment with Sasha Marshall at 8:00 a.m. tomorrow" and provide the relevant information or action.

Wolfram Alpha

Wolfram Alpha is defined as a "computational knowledge engine" which, unlike search engines, provides direct answers to your questions rather than a list of web pages. Search "England versus Brazil" on Wolfram Alpha and Google to examine the differences between the two countries. Because "football" is the most popular search term, even if you don't use "football" as a keyword, Google returns World Cup results. However, as you asked, Alpha would offer you a comprehensive comparison of the two countries. And this is the main difference between web 2.0 and 3.0.

Web 3.0, Cryptocurrency and Blockchain

We may anticipate significant convergence and symbiotic interaction between these three technologies and other disciplines, as web 3.0 networks will be built on decentralized protocols – the underlying technology of Blockchain and cryptocurrency. They will be interoperable, easily integrated, and automated via smart contracts. They will be used to power everything from microtransactions in Africa to censorship-resistant peer-to-peer data storage and sharing via applications like Filecoin to completely transform how businesses operate. The current deluge of DeFi protocols is simply the start.

Top Web 3.0 Projects in 2022

The following are the prominent crypto and Blockchain project gaining massive attention in Web 3.0:

Cirus

Cirus bridges the gap between data and web 3.0 by enabling users to convert their data to Bitcoin and use it as a portal to the new digital economy. Cirus flips the script on large corporations who collect your data for free and sell it for billions. Also, customers can control, monetize, and earn from their data - the way it should be - by employing a suite of services ranging from a web browser extension to mobile applications to a wifi router that supercharges data monetization.

Data is on the verge of becoming the future's most valuable asset, integrated into web 3.0 and the Metaverse to enable new services, financial opportunities, and entirely new types of markets beyond monetization. With Cirus, you'll control this asset and be able to integrate it directly into a web 3.0 platform, enabling you to take advantage of all of these possibilities while also creating a passive investment - your data. Cirus has already developed a Chrome plugin that allows users to begin earning money from their data instantly. Additionally, a large ISP has placed an order for one million routers. Cirus looks to be the best solution for introducing millions of people to web 3.0.

Frontier

Web 3.0 is gaining traction, and many individuals use NFTs and DeFi. Consumers may easily use DeFi and NFTs using Frontier's mobile app. Frontier is a cryptocurrency and distributed ledger technology wallet that enables users to send, store, and invest in over 4000 unique assets. Earn passive income by staking crypto assets, tracking NFTs, and exploring web 3.0 apps all in one place. Frontier supports popular Blockchains like Ethereum, Polygon, Avalanche, Harmony, and BSC, enabling users to keep track of the newest Blockchains while traveling.

Libre DeFi

Nowadays, there is no limit to what we can achieve with DeFi, and Libre DeFi is at the forefront. On the libredefi.io platform, functionalities like token swapping, yield farming, governance, and stablecoins are offered. The number of services available to users in web 3.0 and beyond will continue to grow, and LibreDeFi promised to be up-to-date.

The firm intends to provide NFT boosts as part of its DeFi ecosystem and Farming-as-a-Service (FaaS) as a business-to-business partner proposition, an IDO Launchpad for new token allocations, and a Play-2-Earn gaming experience (P2E). This shows that LibreDeFi will continue to be important in the DeFi industry as web 3.0 evolves.

Bird

The coming of Web 3.0 has implications not just for customers and their overall experience but also for Blockchain developers. Bird addresses this industry gap by providing extensive analytic data to dApp developers via its on-chain oracle. Web 3.0 will give Blockchain developers the tools necessary to build decentralized applications (dApps) and solutions that emulate a more customized user experience, similar to what users are accustomed to on web 2.0 platforms. According to the firm, predictive analytics and Blockchain development may work in tandem to determine the future of Blockchains and the internet. As a result, users will have a web 3.0-specific user experience, ensuring blockchain's future relevance.

420 DAO

When it comes to web 3.0, decentralization is the name of the game, and few technologies have the potential to catapult the industry to new heights, quite like Decentralized Autonomous Organizations (DAO). Because DAOs are likely to play a significant role in web 3.0, 420 DAO ensure that the sector maintains a high level of quality and diversity.

Through their in-house development team and DAO treasury, 420 DAO will aid in the design and funding of critical breakthrough web 3.0 apps. While all DAOs include a commercial component, the 420 DAO distinguishes itself by focusing on good public activities. All proposals will be decentralized from the outset, and community members will vote on them, guaranteeing the most democratic transition possible to web 3.0.

Best Web 3.0 Tokens for 2022
Kusama

Kusama is an open-source, scalable Blockchain network. The Substrate framework is used to create its customized Blockchains. Kusama is a platform enabling Blockchain developers to express themselves and transform their ideas into reality. The network embraces the principles of upending the current quo and redistributing power to people. Kusama was established by Gavin Wood, the co-founder of Ethereum and Polkadot. KSM, the network's token, lets you vote on governance referendums, nominate validators, validate the network, and bond parachains. KSM's current price ranges from $170 to $374, with a market capitalization of $1.4 billion. KSM is expected to reach $4,581.970 by 2026, according to WalletInvestor.

Theta

Theta is a video streaming network that pays people to share their excess bandwidth and computational power. According to Steve Chen, a co-founder of YouTube, Theta will disrupt the internet video market in the same manner that YouTube did in 2005, but differently. By lowering prices, Theta solves the challenge of transmitting video to specific portions of the world. Quality is also not compromised. Theta thinks that everyone should have access to high-quality streaming.

When users share their bandwidth and computational resources, they are rewarded with the TFUEL token. The standard Theta token

(THETA) is tied to the platform's governance. Theta is an open-source platform that enables community creativity, allowing for community innovation. Proof of stake (PoS) and multi-level Byzantine fault tolerance (BFT) are used to protect the network. Theta has a market valuation of $2.56 billion and is now trading at $2.56.

Arweave

Arweave is a decentralized storage network that permits you to store data and apps indefinitely. Your information is kept on a shared hard drive that never forgets. No one can overwrite your data, which is one of the advantages of this design. 404 errors, poor quality in online apps, and stealth modifications are among the other issues that Arweave addresses. AR tokens are awarded for assisting in the upkeep of Arweave's permaweb. Arweave is a community-run business. Other options for remuneration include renting extra storage space and developing a network application.

Arweave is now trading at $33, with slightly over a $1 billion market capitalization. The network employs block weave technology, a Blockchain variant that connects each new block to the one before it and to a random preceding block. Coinbase Ventures, Andreessen Horowitz, and Union Square Ventures have invested in the network.

Siacoin

SC is a web 3.0 coin that you should consider if you wish to support the decentralized internet. Sia offers another data storage option. This technology allows you to manage your encryption keys while storing your data in the cloud across a decentralized network. Sia is less expensive than other cloud storage solutions, with 1 TB of storage costing approximately $1–$2 per month. The platform's cryptocurrency, Siacoin, is used to compensate hosts for providing extra hard drive space for storage. SC may be obtained by mining and trade. With a market capitalization of $0.46 billion, its current price is about $0.0092.

Flux

Flux is a decentralized cloud architecture that is scalable (not to be confused with other companies of the same name). With the benefits of being decentralized, this cloud software competes with IT heavyweights like Amazon Web Services. Flux allows developers to develop, manage, host, and deploy web 3.0 applications across numerous servers at fast rates. For governance, parallel assets, and economics, the Flux Blockchain is employed.

FluxOS, a decentralized operating system, is also available from Flux. Anyone may run a node for the platform, and you'll be paid in a 50/50 split with GPU miners. With the new agreement with tech titans Nvidia on its development, Flux crypto is turning up web 3.0. Flux will benefit from the agreement since it will have unique access to Nvidia's developers and marketers, who will help create a decentralized internet. Flux is now trading at $1.46, with a market value of $327 million.

Ocean Protocol

Ocean Protocol is a cryptocurrency to look into if you want to invest in this field because it gives tools for building web 3.0 apps. Ocean Protocol also decentralizes internet data sharing and access. The OCEAN token is used to buy and sell data and manage community financing. It's meant to grow in size as the number of users grows. The token's supply is also spread overtime to foster long-term stability and short-term growth. OCEAN is now trading at $0.5775 and has a market capitalization of $354 million.

Web 3.0 Companies and Investment Stocks

Web 3.0 looks to be focused on recovering control from large businesses. In recent years, Blockchain technology, which was introduced into our daily lives via cryptocurrencies led by Bitcoin (CCC: BTC-USD), has enabled internet users to decentralize power structures built mainly by big tech.

If you're planning on investing in the web 3.0 space, consider the following seven web 3.0 stocks for long-term profits:

- Advanced Micro Devices (NASDAQ:AMD)
- Block (NYSE:SQ)
- Apple (NASDAQ:AAPL)
- Coinbase Global (NASDAQ:COIN)
- Twitter (NYSE:TWTR)
- Nvidia (NASDAQ:NVDA)
- Unity Software (NYSE:U)

How Brands Can Prepare for Web 3.0

Early-stage applications of the Spatial Web, often known as web 3.0, are already accessible, despite appearances. CEOs must comprehend what the future computer era comprises, how it will impact firms, and how it will create new value as it progresses. Additionally, consumers must be prepared to grasp how some of the more established and experimental web 3.0 business models may collect value in the future years by analyzing existing and practical web 3.0 business models. The sections that follow detail many of the techniques.

Issuing a Native Asset

The value of these native assets is derived from the security they provide; by providing a sufficiently high incentive for real miners to provide hashing power, the cost for malicious actors to conduct an attack increases in lockstep with the price of the native asset, and the added security increases demand of the currency, thereby increasing its price and value. As a result, the indigenous assets' worth has been meticulously appraised and measured.

By acquiring the indigenous asset, you may establish a network. Several of the early crypto network companies had a singular objective: to grow the profitability and worth of their networks. The economic plan was "Grow their local asset treasury; develop the environment." As one of the primary Bitcoin Core maintainers, Blockstream relies on its BTC balance sheet to generate revenue. Meanwhile, ConsenSys has expanded to over 1,000 personnel and is focused on developing crucial infrastructure for the Ethereum (ETH) ecosystem to improve the value of the ETH it owns.

Payment Tokens

With the advent of the token sale, a new generation of Blockchain projects has built their business models on payment tokens inside networks, enabling the creation of two-sided marketplaces and demanding the usage of a native token for all transactions. According to the assumptions, as the network's economy grows, demand for the restricted native payment token will increase, resulting in a rise in the token's value.

Burn Tokens

Firms and projects that form communities via the use of a token may not always be able to distribute earnings to token holders directly. For example, buybacks/token burning have garnered considerable attention as a feature of the Binance (BNB) and MakerDAO (MKR) tokens. As revenue is generated (through Binance trading fees and MakerDAO stability fees), Native tokens are repurchased from the open market and burnt, reducing the total number of tokens and increasing their price.

Taxation of Speculation

The subsequent business models concentrated on establishing the financial infrastructure necessary to support these local assets, such as exchanges, custodians, and derivatives suppliers. They were all formed with the same objective: to provide services to those interested in trading these high-risk products. Because the underlying networks are open and permissionless, organizations like Coinbase cannot establish a monopolistic position by providing "exclusive access." Nonetheless, such businesses' liquidity and branding build defensive moats over time.

Takeaways

- Web 3.0 is a 'in-the-making' future internet version built on public Blockchains, a record-keeping technology best known for enabling bitcoin transactions.

- Web 3.0 is appealing because it is decentralized, instead of customers accessing the internet through services mediated by firms like Google, Apple, or Facebook, individuals control and regulate areas of the internet themselves.

- Web 2.0 is often called the interactive read-write web and the social web. In the web 2.0 ecosystem, you don't have to be a developer to participate in the development process. Many applications are built in such a way that anybody can make them.

- Web 1.0 refers to the first version of the internet. Consider the read-only or syntactic web to be web 1.0. Most of the participants were content consumers, whereas the creators were mostly web developers who produced websites with mostly text or graphics-based content.

- 3D Graphics, Ubiquity, Semantic Web and Artificial Intelligence are the four essential features of web 3.0

- We may anticipate significant convergence and symbiotic interaction between web 3.0, cryptocurrency and blockchain technology and other disciplines, as web 3.0 networks will be built on decentralized protocols – the underlying technology of Blockchain and cryptocurrency. They will be interoperable, easily integrated, and automated via smart contracts.

CHAPTER 12

5G+

Blockchain Potential for 5G

Blockchain and 5G are the most talked-about and hyped technologies in the industry regarding future and fully-fledged technology. The majority of enterprises and organizations have already accepted these new technologies, while just a handful have yet to do so. It'll be fascinating to see how Blockchain will affect the telecommunications business and what obstacles the technology will encounter as it evolves.

When discussing Blockchain and 5G as a whole, it's critical to understand how the two technologies interact. By 2030, Blockchain combination with 5G is predicted to accomplish wonders, connecting about 500 million mobile devices. Because Blockchain is immutable and follows decentralized transaction ledgers, it can facilitate large-scale communication without jeopardizing security, ensuring that organizations and enterprises can trust one another. Because we're all familiar with the properties of Blockchain technology, it's easy to see how these traits might help 5G networks expand and adapt.

Decentralization

Blockchain technology performs transactions without the involvement of a third party or contributors; as a result, it is a decentralized system that eliminates the need for trusted external authority in 5G networking. The decentralizing method also reduces bottlenecks, resulting in more effective service delivery.

Localized Access

We're all aware of Blockchain's transparency, and incorporating it into 5G gives service providers and users complete access to transactions that can be tracked and verified by an authorized individual.

Methodology for Saving Money

Because Blockchain is based on peer-to-peer technology, it eliminates the need for a third-party agreement, resulting in cost savings, improved coordination, and confidence among partners, me, and conflict savings.

Identity Protection

Cryptography is used in Blockchain, implying that all data is encrypted and safeguarded. The marriage of Blockchain with 5G has the potential to alter privacy by enabling distributed trust models, allowing 5G to protect itself against security breaches. Asymmetric cryptography and several hash algorithms are used in Decentralized Blockchain to safeguard the identity of users. The gadgets may be registered with their Blockchain addresses via Blockchain; therefore, there is no identity theft risk.

Best 5G Stock in 2022

The expansion of 5G will help semiconductor businesses, makers of mobile tech equipment and infrastructure, and real estate asset owners—several 5G exchange-traded funds (ETFs) target firms developing the next generation of mobile technology. T-Mobile (NASDAQ: TMUS), as well as competitors Verizon (NYSE: VZ) and AT&T (NYSE: T), are all excellent 5G investments, but investors seeking a higher level of development should look to firms that offer infrastructure, equipment, and technology. Therefore, we have prepared a fine list of promising options of 5G stocks for your future investment.

Corning

5G data, like all electronic data, must go over the wired section of the internet before being converted into a high-speed Wi-Fi signal. Fiber-optic cable fills the gap, and Corning, a long-established glass and ceramics company, is a significant provider. Many companies delivering 5G services will need to add extra high-speed cable to their networks and build new radio towers. Corning also manufactures small cell antennas and software, which are key components of 5G systems used to distribute wireless signals in office buildings and sports arenas. Corning has a lengthy history in the industry., but it has a history of increasing its dividend payments to shareholders.

Ciena

Ciena is another firm that supplies communications companies with fiber-optic equipment and network design services. Ciena has been able to pay down debt, raise cash reserves, and repurchase stock thanks to income generated by the expansion of 5G technology. It has created additional skills along the road, including a software section that assists telcos with network management. The firm is capable of supplying the engineering design and materials needed to enable next-generation mobility as enterprises upgrade their systems to support 5G. Ciena is back in growth after a sales downturn early in the COVID-19 epidemic.

Arista Networks

Arista Networks, a data center, and internet infrastructure business, is a frequently neglected 5G stock. Data centers will play an increasingly essential role in mobile network management since 5G may transmit large quantities of data, allowing ultra-high-definition video streaming or communications for network-connected cars. Arista is a leading data center equipment vendor, offering open-source hardware, administration, and cybersecurity technologies. As 5G expands the capabilities of mobile devices, Arista is well-positioned to gain from the associated surge in cloud computing services.

5G Real Estate Investment

Real estate is also required for 5G. To transmit 5G signals, towers and other fixed assets are needed, and real estate investment trusts (REITs) such as American Tower, Crown Castle, and Digital Realty Trust are among the prominent participants in the market.

American Tower

American Tower is a leading tech real estate business and one of the significant REITs. It has about 220,000 assets globally and focuses on land, buildings, and cell tower sites critical to mobile networks and internet infrastructure operation. It also creates fiber-optic networks to connect 5G small cell sites to the rest of the internet, a key service for mobile network operators as more consumers and companies rely on mobile services for internet access.

The Royal Castle

Crown Castle is a significantly smaller company than American Tower, yet it manages a significant portion of North America's communications infrastructure. It has over 40,000 cell towers, tens of thousands of kilometers of fiber, and a rapidly expanding portfolio of tiny cell nodes for a 5G rollout. While businesses are expanding faster than real estate, Crown Castle provides its stockholders with the opportunity for development as the 5G industry grows while also giving out dividends.

Digital Realty Trust

Digital Realty Trust is a leading developer and acquirer of data centers, the industry's basic processing units. Because cloud services and 5G overlap, it's important noting that Digital Realty's clients include telecoms firms constructing the physical assets that will enable 5G. Even though their investments are primarily intended to generate income, the share prices of all three REITs have increased dramatically over the last decade. The demand for Crown Castle, American Tower, and Digital Realty Trust real estate assets will further increase as mobility becomes more vital and data volume expands.

Takeaways

- 5G is known as the fifth generation of wireless networking technology. It has decreased latency (the time between an input or data request and the network's response) and downloads speeds up to 100 times quicker than 4G.

- While past telecom network improvements facilitated smartphones and mobility booms, 5G technology further ingests digital technology into everyday life.

- Investing in 5G-focused firms carries the same risks as any other investment.

CONCLUSION

A Blockchain is a system in which digital asset transactions are recorded in data blocks that are "chained" together in a precise sequence and secured by complicated computer "hash" algorithms. Before another transaction can be entered into the ledger, its details must be validated by a network of computers called nodes.

Blockchain technology is comparable to distributed ledger technology (DLT), but it is unique to cryptocurrency and the many technologies that have emerged from it. Blockchain technology employs cryptography and verification mechanisms to limit access to append-only, meaning that new data may be input, but previous data cannot be modified. Blockchain applications have increased, with the technology being used in anything from tokenizing pixel art such as in NFTs to fantasy football competitions and digital worlds where you can purchase a piece of virtual real estate like in Metaverse.

You may put your money into various firms exploring and creating blockchain and DLT products and services. Many Popular firms, like Meta, Amazon, Apple, Google, IBM and Nvidia are exploring Blockchain applications and technologies, and many more are developing in the public and private sectors. There are various markets from which to choose: Decentralized Finance (DeFi), cryptocurrency, Metaverse, Exchanges, NFTs

Blockchain has enabled the decentralization and tokenization of practically everything of value—a corporation seeking to raise funds may use a Blockchain to construct digital investment instruments, similar to how NFTs are formed. Investing in Blockchain technology does not imply investing in Bitcoin or any other digital asset. Investments can be made in the stock of other firms, through the purchase of ETFs, and through crowdsourcing, among other options. Undoubtedly, Blockchain technology has a promising future and the time to act is now.

Dear Reader,

As independent authors it's often difficult to gather reviews compared with much bigger publishers.

Therefore, please leave a review on the platform where you bought this book.

Many thanks,

Author Team

Want Free New Book Launches?
Email us at:
mindsetmastership@gmail.com

Printed in Great Britain
by Amazon

10927937R00096